The Mediterranean Table

Rena Patten

The Mediterranean Table

Easy to prepare meat, seafood, breads and dips, vegetarian and vegan recipes suitable for everyday meals, or platters and grazing boards to share with friends and family.

NEW HOLLAND

Contents

INTRODUCTION 9

SOUPS 15

BREADS AND DIPS 29

SALADS 53

PASTA & RICE 77

MEAT 97

SEAFOOD 127

POULTRY 165

VEGETARIAN 187

INDEX 223

About the Author

Growing up with a Mediterranean background, cooking and eating were a big event in my household and the food of Greece, Italy, France and the Middle East was a part of everyday life. From a very young age this instilled a great passion in me and I've now been involved with food and cooking for well over 40 years.

I am a home cook and not a trained chef – I attended what I think was the best cookery school and that was our home kitchen where my teachers were my mother and grandmothers. I have a natural understanding and love of food and I am always happy in the kitchen surrounded by lots of fresh ingredients, cooking and creating new recipes.

My mother went to work when I was 13 and she would come home after a long and tiring day and start cooking the food that we loved and had gotten used to over the years. It didn't matter how tired she was she would always prepare a home-cooked meal.

One day I decided to surprise my parents by preparing the evening meal. It was the first proper meal that I prepared on my own and I remember that it was Greek lamb chops with vegetables and Greek salad.

After that I prepared dinner as often as I could every week and it was then that the cooking bug bit and bit really hard. Since having my own family I have loved nothing more than to cook for them. I have always considered it a blessing and a privilege to be able do so, something that I hope I have passed on to my children and grandchildren.

To date I am the published author of 11 cookbooks; I was the first person in Australia, or probably the world I am told, to write a cookbook solely on quinoa. What was supposed to be one book and one book only on quinoa turned out to be four.

I have catered extensively over the years, taught cooking at local colleges and shopping centres, have done interviews on TV and radio, talks at many libraries, private functions, shopping centres and well-known homeware stores. I also had a recipe column with a local newspaper for a number of years.

In 2008 and 2009 I was fortunate enough to be involved with the Good Food and Wine Shows in Melbourne and Sydney and the Lifestyle and Retirement Expo in Sydney where I held cooking demonstrations to sit-down audiences. It was then that my association with New Holland began.

Dedication

For
Graeme,
Mum and Dad

Introduction

Welcome to *The Mediterranean Table,* where in my kitchen food from this wonderful region of the world is prepared on an almost everyday basis.

The Mediterranean diet is regarded as one of the healthiest and most popular in the world. It has earned this accolade because of the health benefits associated with the type of ingredients used, its cooking methods, and for being a diet that is so diverse it can be enjoyed by meat eaters and non-meat eaters alike. Vegetarian and vegan meals feature greatly in the Mediterranean kitchen.

I have a Mediterranean background and was born in a Mediterranean country where I was fortunate enough to be brought up enjoying food from Greece, Italy, France and the Middle East.

The main ingredients in the Mediterranean kitchen are simple and readily available comprising lots of fresh vegetables, fruit, legumes/pulses, whole grains, seafood, smaller amounts of meat and poultry, seeds, nuts, herbs and spices, olive oil and of course garlic. These are the ingredients that make up the foundation of the Mediterranean cuisine.

The recipes in this book are mainly traditional recipes that have been prepared in Mediterranean kitchens for many years. They are the recipes that I grew up with, and I remember my mother and grandmother spending hours in the kitchen preparing delicious and healthy meals. There are a wide variety of dishes that were prepared when I was a child as well as ones that I have prepared for my own family for many years. Some have been simplified without losing the traditional flavour to fit in with today's lifestyle.

Although life has changed and most of us do not have the time to spend hours in the kitchen like our mothers, grandmothers and great-grandmothers did, you will find the recipes in this book easy to prepare using readily available ingredients that are mostly found at the local supermarket.

The wonderful thing about Mediterranean food is that although meals are served and enjoyed as a main meal, a large selection of them are also suitable to be served as mezze (also known as tapas) or on a grazing board to be shared and leisurely enjoyed over a period of time.

Mediterranean cooking and the Mediterranean table are all about fresh home-cooked food and lots of it, cooked with love, shared with family and friends and usually served on big platters that are placed in the middle of the table for everyone to help themselves.

Eating is a very important event in the Mediterranean culture, so much so that I would actually call it a ritual; it is a time where beautiful memories are made, spending time with people we love and sharing food that we love.

Grazing Boards/Mezze/Tapas

Mezze/tapas are very popular in a lot of Mediterranean countries; it is a very common way of enjoying food and a way that makes having a meal a fun experience. They are not a course in a meal such as an appetiser or an entrée, they are a selection of small dishes which become the entire actual meal. These dishes are usually salty, spicy or savoury, can be served hot or cold, and might be enjoyed as a leisurely lunch or dinner, or at any time of the day with or without drinks.

These dishes are perfect to serve on grazing boards. The grazing board is really an adaptation of a mezze/tapas meal, very much like an antipasto platter. The array of food is usually served on a beautiful large wooden board or tray to be shared.

Dishes in this book that are suitable for serving on grazing boards are marked as such as are the vegetarian and vegan meals.

Health Benefits

There have been a lot of studies done on the benefits for those who fully or partially follow a Mediterranean diet. These have shown that the traditional food from the region has huge benefits in controlling certain diseases as well as resulting in an overall feeling of wellness. Eating a Mediterranean diet has been known to lower the risk of certain conditions such as cardiovascular disease, cancer and diabetes to name a few. It can also be beneficial in lowering cholesterol, promoting healthy aging and help establish healthier mental function.

Preparation

You will find all the recipes in this book easy to prepare using ingredients that are readily available from the supermarket, your local delicatessen, green grocer, butcher

or fishmonger. You will not have to travel the world to find them. There are just a few basic things to remember though:

- Firstly, not all cookware, stoves and ovens are the same and so cooking and baking times will vary depending on how your own stove and oven work as well as the type of cookware that you use.
- For the recipes that require grilling or frying, I find a good non-stick griddle pan or frying pan works really well on top of the stove.
- For ease of cleaning I like to line baking trays with non-stick baking paper so that any mess can just be thrown away.
- Most of the recipes in this book have been designed to feed 4–6 or 6–8 people.
- Basic pantry must-haves for Mediterranean cooking are olive oil (preferably extra virgin), onions, garlic (and lots of it), tinned tomatoes, tomato paste, dried and tinned legumes/pulses such as lentils, chickpeas and beans (tinned legumes are great for quick cooking with no long soaking time required and they work beautifully in most dishes), pasta, rice, vinegars, fresh and dried herbs and spices, and fresh lemons and limes.
- The seasoning of food is one of personal taste and differs greatly between people. That is why for the most part I have not specified amounts, I have left that entirely up to you.
- For convenience sake with today's busy lifestyles, I have used ready-made pastry in some recipes that call for the use of pastry. The quality of ready-made pastry available these days is so good that I don't feel it is always warranted for anyone to spend time making their own.
- I tend to use extra-virgin olive oil for just about everything. I love using it and find it adds so much flavour to dishes. I use it for cooking, frying, basting and of course in salads or for that extra drizzle on cooked food.

Happy cooking and I truly hope you have many happy and memorable moments as your travel through my Mediterranean kitchen.

SOUPS

Rustic Beef, Vegetable and Cracked Wheat Soup

SERVES 6

2 tablespoons extra-virgin olive oil
1 onion, finely chopped
1 leek, washed and finely sliced
2 medium potatoes, cubed
2 medium carrots, cubed
2 stalks celery, chopped
2 cloves garlic, chopped
750 g (27 oz) gravy beef, cut into chunks
2 tomatoes, skinned, de-seeded and chopped
2 litres (64 fl oz) beef stock
salt and freshly ground pepper
150 g (5 oz) frozen peas
large handful of fresh baby spinach
125 g (4 oz) cracked wheat/bourghul
250 ml (8 fl oz) boiling water
lemon juice for serving

Heat oil in a large saucepan over medium–high heat and sauté the onion, leek, potatoes, carrots, celery (including some of the more tender celery leaves which have been chopped), and garlic until soft and just starting to take on some colour. Add the beef, tomatoes and stock and season with salt and pepper. Bring to the boil, reduce the heat, cover and simmer on low heat for an hour.

Add the cracked wheat and boiling water, bring back to a full rolling boil, reduce the heat, cover, and continue simmering for another 40 minutes, or until the meat is tender and the soup has thickened.

Stir in the peas and spinach and cook for another 10 minutes.

Take off the heat and leave to stand for 15–20 minutes before serving with crusty bread and a sprinkle of lemon juice. The meat can be pulled apart with two forks into smaller pieces for serving.

Note: This is a hearty and thick soup ideal for the cold winter days. Great for freezing.

Tomato and Basil Soup

SERVES 4

VEGAN

1 tablespoon extra-virgin olive oil
1 large red onion, chopped
3 cloves garlic, chopped
1 tablespoon tomato paste
½ teaspoon sugar
1 teaspoon dried oregano
1 teaspoon dried fennel seeds
800 g (28 oz) can diced tomatoes
1 litre (32 fl oz) beef, chicken or vegetable stock
½ cup fresh basil leaves, chopped
salt and freshly ground black pepper
2 vermicelli nests, broken into small pieces
chives, chopped, to garnish
grated parmesan cheese, to garnish

Heat oil in a large saucepan over medium heat and sauté onion until soft. Stir in the garlic and cook until fragrant. Stir in the tomato paste then add the sugar, oregano and fennel and cook for about a minute. Add the tomatoes, stock and basil leaves, and season with salt and pepper. Bring to the boil, reduce heat, cover and simmer for 20–25 minutes.

Blend soup in a food processor or using a stick blender, add the vermicelli and either take off the heat and leave covered for 20 minutes for the pasta to cook or cook on low heat for about 5 minutes.

Serve topped with chives and grated parmesan. To make the dish vegan omit the cheese or replace with a vegan alternative.

Egyptian Molokhia Soup

SERVES 6

1 large red onion, finely chopped
brown vinegar
4 large chicken thigh cutlets
8 cups water or
 chicken stock
1 carrot, peeled and halved
1 tomato, halved
1 onion, peeled and halved
750 g (27 oz) frozen chopped
 molokhia

Garnish

4 tablespoons extra-virgin olive oil
4–6 cloves garlic, grated
1 heaped tablespoon ground cumin
1 heaped tablespoon ground coriander
sea salt and freshly ground pepper
lemon juice, to serve
boiled rice, to serve

Put the red onion in a bowl, cover with the vinegar and set aside.

Place the chicken, water or stock, carrot, tomato and onion in a large saucepan, bring to the boil, reduce heat, cover and simmer for about 45 minutes, until chicken is cooked and you have a rich stock.

Remove and discard the carrot, tomato and onion. Remove the chicken and set aside until cool enough to shred. Add the molokhia to the stock, bring back to the boil, reduce heat, cover and simmer for 25–30 minutes.

In the meantime prepare the garnish. Heat the oil in a medium-sized frying pan over medium heat and cook the garlic for about 30 seconds until it starts to change colour. Stir in the cumin and coriander and continue cooking for about 1 minute until fragrant. Keep stirring so that the spices do not burn. Remove from the heat and immediately pour into the soup. Add the shredded chicken, stir well and leave to rest for at least 10 minutes before serving to allow the flavours to combine.

Serve over boiled rice and garnish with a little lemon juice and a tablespoon or so of the onion and vinegar.

Note: Molokhia is a very popular Egyptian soup and my mother used to make it when I was a child using fresh molokhia leaves, which can be difficult to find these days. Molokhia is actually a green leafy vegetable, an ancient Egyptian supergreen, like spinach but totally different in appearance and with a distinct taste. These days it is easier and more convenient to find it available in the freezer section of Middle Eastern grocery shops. Another name for molokhia is jute mallow leaves. If you are unable to find molokhia you can substitute silverbeet. You would need the leaves of about two large bunches and they will have to be chopped very finely.

Pumpkin, Lentil and Spinach Soup

SERVES 6

VEGAN

3 tablespoons extra-virgin olive oil
2 onions, roughly chopped
4–5 cloves garlic, roughly chopped
1 tablespoon ground cumin
2 teaspoons ground coriander
1 kg (35 oz) pumpkin, peeled and cut into chunks
200 g (7 oz) red lentils, rinsed
½–1 teaspoon chilli flakes
1.5 litres (50 fl oz) chicken or vegetable stock
150 g (5 oz) baby spinach leaves
salt and freshly ground black pepper
lime juice and Greek/Vegan yoghurt, to serve

Heat oil in a large saucepan over medium–high heat and sauté onion until golden. Stir in the garlic and cook until fragrant. Stir in the cumin and coriander and cook for about a minute making sure the spices don't burn. Add the pumpkin, lentils, chilli and stock. Bring to the boil then reduce the heat and simmer for 30–35 minutes, until the lentils are cooked.

Remove from the heat and puree the soup either in a food processor or using a stick blender. Return soup to the heat, bring back to the boil, stir in the spinach and season with salt and pepper.

Switch off the heat and allow to stand for 5–10 minutes before serving with lime juice and a dollop of Greek/Vegan yoghurt.

Brown Lentil and Spinach Soup

SERVES 6

VEGAN

375 g (13 oz) dried brown lentils
3 tablespoons extra-virgin olive oil
2 large onions, finely chopped
4–6 large cloves garlic, finely chopped
2 tablespoons finely grated fresh ginger
2 heaped teaspoons ground cumin
1½ teaspoons ground coriander
1½ teaspoons curry powder
2 teaspoons sweet paprika
1 tablespoon tomato paste
chilli flakes to taste
2 litres (64 fl oz) water or vegetable stock
120 g (4 oz) baby spinach leaves
lime juice, Greek/Vegan yoghurt and chopped fresh coriander (cilantro) to serve
salt and pepper

Pick over the lentils to remove any small stones or grit then rinse thoroughly under cold running water in a fine sieve. Place in a large saucepan, cover with water, bring to the boil and simmer for 10–12 minutes. Drain and rinse lentils then set aside.

Heat the oil in a large saucepan over medium–high heat and sauté onion until golden. Stir in the garlic and ginger and cook for about 30 seconds, until fragrant. Add the cumin, coriander, curry powder and paprika, stir well and continue cooking for one minute. Stir in the tomato paste and chilli flakes and cook for another minute. Add the lentils and water or stock, bring to the boil, reduce the heat, cover and simmer for one hour or until lentils are tender. You may need to add more water or stock, depending on how thick you like your soup. Stir in the spinach and season with salt and pepper. Cook for 3 minutes until spinach has wilted.

Serve with a good squeeze of lime juice, Greek/Vegan yoghurt and a sprinkle of fresh coriander.

Black-Eyed Bean Soup

SERVES 6

VEGAN

375 g (13 oz) dried black-eyed beans
2 tablespoons extra-virgin olive oil
1 large onion, chopped
4 cloves garlic, chopped
1 tablespoon tomato paste
2 medium carrots, diced
1 celery stalk with leaves, stalk diced and leaves chopped
400 g (14 oz) can diced tomatoes
1.5 litres (50 fl oz) water
2 medium zucchini (courgettes), diced
3–4 tablespoons chopped flat-leaf parsley
salt and freshly ground black pepper

Place the beans in a large saucepan and cover with cold water. Bring to the boil then reduce heat and cook for 10 minutes. Remove from heat, drain, rinse and set aside.

Heat the oil in a large saucepan over medium–high heat, sauté the onion until soft and golden then stir in the garlic and cook until fragrant. Stir in the tomato paste, cook for about a minute then add the beans, carrot, celery, diced tomatoes and water. Bring to the boil, reduce the heat, cover and simmer for 45–50 minutes. Add the zucchini and parsley, season with salt and pepper and continue cooking for another 15–20 minutes until beans and vegetables are tender.

Adjust seasoning to taste and serve with crusty bread.

Note: Unlike other beans, black-eyed beans do not need to be soaked before using. This is a thick, hearty and nutritious soup. Ideal for those cold wintery days, traditionally this soup, is served with bread and chopped fresh onion. Great for freezing.

Cauliflower Soup

SERVES 6

2 tablespoons extra-virgin olive oil
1 large onion, finely chopped
½ small cauliflower, about 500 g (18 oz), cut into small pieces
400 g (14 oz) can diced tomatoes
1 large potato, peeled and diced into small pieces
1.5 litres (50 fl oz) chicken or vegetable stock
60 g (2 oz) small pasta/macaroni
salt and pepper
2 eggs, lightly beaten
60 g (2 oz) grated parmesan cheese
handful finely chopped parsley
shaved parmesan cheese

Heat oil in a large saucepan over medium–high heat and sauté onion until soft then add the cauliflower, tomatoes, potatoes and stock. Bring to the boil then reduce heat, cover and simmer for 15 minutes. Stir in the pasta, season with salt and pepper and continue cooking for another 12–15 minutes until pasta is cooked. In the meantime stir the parmesan cheese into the beaten egg and mix well.

Take the soup off the heat and leave to stand uncovered for five minutes. Stir in the egg and cheese mixture a little at a time, stirring continuously, until all the egg mixture is used and the soup thickens. Stir in the parsley, adjust the seasoning if necessary and leave for a further 5 minutes before serving with parmesan cheese and crusty bread. The pasta will continue to absorb stock and thicken the soup the longer it stands before serving.

Note: My grandmother used to make this soup often when I was a child; it was so delicious and satisfying on a cold winter's day. She sometimes used peas instead of the potato.

Spiced Red Lentil Soup

SERVES 6

VEGAN

400 g (14 oz) dried red lentils
1.75 litres (52 fl oz) water
2 fresh tomatoes, quartered
1 large onion, chopped
2 cloves garlic, chopped
1 bay leaf
2 tablespoons olive oil
salt and pepper to taste

Garnish

80 ml (2½ fl oz) extra-virgin olive oil
1 medium onion, very finely chopped
4 large cloves garlic, grated or very finely chopped
1½ tablespoons ground cumin
1 tablespoon ground coriander
sliced red chilli and croutons to serve

Pick over the lentils to remove any small stones or grit then rinse under cold running water in a fine sieve until the water runs clear. Put the lentils in a large saucepan with the water, tomatoes, onion, garlic, bay leaf, olive oil, salt and pepper. Bring to the boil then reduce the heat, cover and simmer on low heat for 30–40 minutes until the lentils are tender and the soup has thickened. Skim and discard any foam that appears on the surface while cooking.

When the soup is ready, remove from the heat and remove the tomato skins and bay leaf. Puree until smooth then return to the stove on low heat.

Prepare the garnish by heating the oil in a frying pan over medium heat and sauté the onion until it's a deep golden colour. Add the garlic and cook for a minute until fragrant, stir in the cumin and coriander, cook for another minute until the spices have released their oils and are fragrant, being careful not to burn.

Stir garnish into the soup, mix well and heat through before serving with a drizzle of extra-virgin olive oil, slices of chilli and croutons, if using.

Borlotti Bean and Vegetable Soup

SERVES 6

VEGAN

500 g (18 oz) dried borlotti beans
3 tablespoons extra-virgin olive oil
1 large onion, finely chopped
4 medium carrots, cubed into small pieces
4 stalks celery, strings removed and chopped
5 cloves garlic, finely chopped
2 medium potatoes, cubed into small pieces
400 g (14 oz) can diced tomatoes
2 tablespoons chopped fresh rosemary
1 tablespoon chopped fresh thyme
1 tablespoon chopped fresh oregano
2 litres (64 fl oz) vegetable or chicken stock
300 g (11 oz) finely sliced cabbage
salt and freshly ground pepper to taste
handful finely chopped flat-leaf parsley
grated parmesan cheese (or vegan substitute)

Soak the beans in plenty of cold water for 24 hours. They will expand to around three times their original size.

Heat oil in a large heavy saucepan over medium–high heat, add the onion, carrot and celery including some of the more tender leaves, and cook until soft and just starting to change colour. Stir in the garlic and cook until fragrant then add the potatoes, tomatoes and herbs and cook for 1–2 minutes. Add the drained beans and stock, bring to the boil then reduce the heat, cover and simmer for one hour.

Stir in the cabbage and continue simmering for another 30–45 minutes, until the beans are tender. Switch off the heat, season with salt and pepper and stir in the parsley. Serve with a good sprinkle of grated parmesan cheese.

Note: If you have any parmesan cheese rind in your fridge, pop it in the soup while it is cooking. If you want an even thicker soup add some little pasta such as small ditti or macaroni at the same time as the cabbage.

BREADS & DIPS

Hummus

SERVES 4 VEGAN SUITABLE FOR GRAZING BOARD

400 g (14 oz) can chickpeas (garbanzos), drained and rinsed
100 ml (3½ fl oz) water (approx.)
60 g (2 oz) tahini paste
2 cloves garlic, finely grated
60 ml (2 fl oz) lemon juice
3 teaspoons extra-virgin olive oil
salt and freshly ground black pepper to taste
extra-virgin olive oil
ground sweet paprika

Place chickpeas and water into a mini food processor and process until smooth. Add the tahini paste, garlic, lemon juice, oil, salt and pepper, and process until you get a smooth puree. Taste and adjust seasoning if necessary.

To serve, spread hummus into a shallow serving dish, drizzle some extra-virgin olive oil on top and sprinkle with paprika.

Note: Sometimes tahini paste can be quite thick depending on the brand you use. If you find the hummus is too thick just add a little extra water or lemon juice.

Baba Ganoush (Eggplant/Aubergine Dip)

SERVES 4 VEGAN SUITABLE FOR GRAZING BOARD

- 1 large eggplant (aubergine), about 500 g (18 oz)
- 1–2 cloves garlic, very finely grated
- 80 ml (2½ fl oz) tahini paste
- 80 ml (2½ fl oz) lemon juice
- 1 tablespoon extra-virgin olive oil
- salt and freshly ground black pepper
- 2 tablespoons finely chopped flat-leaf parsley

Preheat oven to 190°C (375°F) and line a baking tray with non-stick baking paper.

Grill eggplant on a cake rack over a gas hob for about 10 minutes turning a few times (the skin will blacken and give the eggplant that smoky taste) then place on the baking tray to finish cooking in the oven until soft, about 25–30 minutes. Alternatively, if you don't have a gas cook top, place eggplant in the centre shelf of a preheated oven and bake until soft and skin blackens, about 35–45 minutes.

While still hot, cut through the eggplant skin and with a spoon, remove the flesh and chop very finely then give it a really good stir with a fork. Stir in the garlic, tahini, lemon juice and oil, season with salt and pepper and mix well. Stir in the parsley and serve in a shallow dish with a drizzle of extra-virgin olive oil.

Note: Traditionally eggplant is chargrilled over an open fire until the skin starts to blister. This takes about 30–40 minutes turning frequently. If you have the time to do this it is well worth it as the baba ganoush will have that delicious and traditional slightly smoky flavour. I find you get a similar effect by using the method above using a gas hob.

Tzatziki (Cucumber Dip)

SERVES 4–6

SUITABLE FOR GRAZING BOARD

3 medium Lebanese cucumbers
salt
300 g (11 oz) thick Greek yoghurt
½ teaspoon brown vinegar
2 teaspoons extra-virgin olive oil
2 cloves garlic, very finely grated
1½ teaspoons dried mint leaves
1–2 teaspoons chopped fresh mint leaves
salt and freshly ground black pepper

Coarsely grate the unpeeled cucumbers and place in a fine sieve, sprinkle with a little salt then squeeze with your hands to remove as much liquid as you can. Leave to drain for about 20 minutes. After 20 minutes, squeeze again to remove any excess moisture (you will be amazed at just how much liquid comes out of the cucumbers!).

Place the yoghurt in a bowl with the cucumbers, vinegar, oil, garlic, mint, salt and pepper and mix well. Check seasoning and adjust if necessary. Refrigerate for at least 3 hours before serving, preferably overnight.

Note: Tzatziki is a very popular dip that is a great accompaniment to a lot of dishes and is particularly delicious with grilled lamb. It is also served as a side salad.

Ricotta, Olive and Basil Tart with Tomatoes

SERVES 4–6

SUITABLE FOR GRAZING BOARD

375 g (13 oz) frozen puff pastry, thawed
350 g (12 oz) ricotta cheese
2–3 tablespoons grated parmesan
125 g (4 oz) pitted kalamata olives, halved
1 tablespoon finely grated lemon zest
1 tablespoon lemon juice
1 tablespoon extra-virgin olive oil
1–2 cloves garlic, finely grated or chopped
1 teaspoon dried oregano leaves
handful of chopped basil
half bunch fresh chives, chopped
2 eggs, lightly beaten

Dressing

500 g (18 oz) medley cherry tomatoes
125 ml (4 fl oz) extra-virgin olive oil
1 tablespoon red wine or balsamic vinegar
1 teaspoon dried oregano leaves
salt and freshly ground black pepper
basil leaves and chopped chives

Preheat oven to 200°C (400°F).

Line a 26 x 35 cm (10 x 14 in) baking tray with non-stick baking paper. Top with one and a half sheets of the pastry (if using ready rolled pastry sheets) joining the two ends together to make one large sheet or alternatively roll out a single sheet of pastry.

Combine ricotta, parmesan, olives, lemon zest, lemon juice, oil, garlic, herbs, and most of the beaten egg and season with salt and a generous amount of freshly ground pepper. Spread mixture over pastry, leaving a 2 cm (¾ in) border. Brush border lightly with remaining egg then bake, for 15–20 minutes, rotating the tray if needed, until pastry is golden all over.

While the tart is baking make the dressing by combining the tomatoes, oil, vinegar and oregano and season to taste. Pile the tomato dressing on top of the baked tart, garnish with herbs and serve warm.

Olive, Spinach and Feta Twist

SERVES 4–6

SUITABLE FOR GRAZING BOARD

olive paste

180 g (6 oz) pitted kalamata olives
1 teaspoon dried oregano leaves
1 tablespoon extra-virgin olive oil
1–2 cloves garlic, chopped
2 tablespoons chopped flat-leaf parsley

dough

350 g (12 oz) plain flour
1½ teaspoons salt
2 teaspoons dried oregano leaves
2 teaspoons active yeast powder
1 large egg
80 ml (2½ fl oz) extra-virgin olive oil
150 ml (5 fl oz) water
1 quantity olive paste
small handful spinach
60 g (2 oz) Greek feta
sesame seeds

Note: Chilli flakes can be added to the olive paste for a burst of heat.

To make the olive paste: Place all the ingredients in a food processor and process until you have a paste.

Sift flour and salt into a bowl then mix in the oregano and yeast. Make a well in the centre, add the egg, oil and water and mix to bring dough together. Either knead with your hands for a good 10 minutes or put all the ingredients into a stand mixer and using the dough hook attachment knead for 5–7 minutes. Put the dough in an oiled bowl, cover with plastic wrap and leave until doubled in size, about 2 hours.

Line a large baking tray with non-stick paper. When the dough has doubled in size, knock out the air and with your hands shape into a rectangle (this facilitates rolling). Place onto a lightly floured surface and roll out into a rectangle about 30 x 45 cm (11–18 in). With the longer side of the dough facing you spread the olive paste all over the dough, top with the spinach leaves pressing them into the paste then crumble the feta all over. Lightly press the toppings into the dough.

Tightly roll up the dough to form a long sausage shape. Squeeze the roll tightly together then using a sharp knife cut the dough all the way down the centre of the roll, leaving a small area at the top of the roll intact to hold it together. Turn the two pieces upward to expose the filling then slowly twist together. Press the ends together then carefully place onto the prepared tray, loosely cover with plastic wrap and leave to rise for about an hour.

Preheat oven to 200°C (400°F). Sprinkle the twist with some sesame seeds and bake for about 35–40 minutes. Remove from the oven and brush all over with a little extra-virgin olive oil.

Italian Pizza Loaf

SERVES 4–6

SUITABLE FOR GRAZING BOARD

2 large green capsicums (peppers)
3 tablespoons extra-virgin olive oil
1 tablespoon balsamic vinegar
1 Italian ring-shaped bread loaf
250 g (9 oz) tasty or gruyere cheese, sliced
2–3 large ripe tomatoes, thickly sliced
1 red onion, thinly sliced
freshly ground black pepper
12 black olives, halved and seeded
125 g (4 oz) Italian salami, sliced
300 g (11 oz) grated mozzarella cheese
2 tablespoons freshly grated parmesan cheese
1 teaspoon dried oregano leaves

Preheat oven to 190°C (375°F).

Place whole capsicums under a hot grill until the skin has blackened all over, but do not burn. Place into a plastic bag for about 10 minutes (this helps make it easier to remove the skins). Peel off skins, discard seeds and cut into thick strips. Place in a dish and drizzle with olive oil and vinegar.

Slice a lid off the top of the bread and remove most of the inside. Place three-quarters of the cheese at the bottom of the bread and top with capsicum then layer the tomato and onion and sprinkle with ground pepper and any of the leftover dressing from the capsicums. Top with olives and salami then the remaining tasty/gruyere cheese.

Combine the mozzarella, parmesan and oregano then sprinkle on top. Replace the bread lid, lightly press together and place on a baking tray and bake for approximately 20 minutes. Cut into wedges and serve.

Sun-Dried Tomato, Herb and Garlic Cheese Ball

SERVES 6–8

SUITABLE FOR GRAZING BOARD

250 g (9 oz) cream cheese at room temperature
2 cloves garlic, very finely grated
45 g (1½ oz) semi-dried tomatoes, finely chopped
2 teaspoons lemon juice
salt
freshly ground black pepper
1 bunch chives, finely chopped
½ bunch flat-leaf parsley, finely chopped

Place cream cheese in a bowl and mix with a fork until smooth. Add the garlic, sun-dried tomatoes, lemon juice, salt and pepper and mix thoroughly until well combined. Place cheese ball onto a piece of plastic cling film and wrap tightly to form a ball. Refrigerate for at least 24 hours, preferably 48 hours.

On the day of serving, mix the chives and parsley together then roll the cheese ball in the herbs, lightly pressing as you go, until completely covered. Refrigerate until ready to serve.

Serve with slices of toasted baguette or crackers.

Pizza Wheels

MAKES 50–55 WHEELS

SUITABLE FOR GRAZING BOARD

300 g (11 oz) pitted kalamata olives
2 tablespoons tomato paste
3 cloves garlic, chopped
125 g (4 oz) grated parmesan cheese
1 tablespoon dried oregano leaves
handful chopped flat-leaf parsley
freshly ground black pepper
2 tablespoons extra-virgin olive oil
5 sheets ready rolled puff pastry
1 egg, beaten
sesame seeds

Preheat oven to 190°C (375°F) and line two baking trays with non-stick baking paper.

Place the olives, tomato paste, garlic, parmesan, oregano, parsley, pepper and olive oil into a food processor and process until you get a thick paste. Spread the olive paste all over each pastry sheet starting from the bottom end closest to you, leaving a 2 cm (¾ in) border at the top end. Fold over and roll up to a firm roll. Cut each roll into 2 cm (¾ in) slices and place on the tray.

Brush the tops and sides of the pizza wheels with the beaten egg, sprinkle with sesame seeds and bake for about 15–20 minutes until puffed and golden.

Note: These are great to have on hand in the freezer. You can prepare them up to the stage where they are rolled then wrap in plastic film and freeze. Take out of the freezer as you need them, defrost slightly, cut into slices, brush with egg, sprinkle with sesame seeds and bake.

Olive Bread

SERVES 6

SUITABLE FOR GRAZING BOARD

3 large eggs
165 ml (5½ fl oz) extra-virgin olive oil
200 g (7 oz) Greek yoghurt
175 g (6 oz) kalamata olives, sliced
6 shallots (scallions/spring onions), sliced
1½ tablespoons dried mint
1 tablespoon salt
freshly ground black pepper
200 g (7 oz) self-raising flour
¾ teaspoon baking powder

Preheat oven to 200°C (400°F) and line a baking tin approximately 34 x 24 cm (13½ x 9½ in) with non-stick baking paper.

Using a whisk, mix the eggs, oil and yoghurt together until well combined. Stir in the olives, shallots, mint, salt and pepper.

Sift flour and baking powder together and add to the egg mixture. Mix well until all the ingredients are well combined – the mixture should be soft. Pour mixture into prepared tin and bake for about 30 minutes until bread is set and top is golden.

Remove from the oven and allow to cool for about 15 minutes before cutting into fingers or squares.

Note: You can add cubes of feta to the mixture.

Mediterranean Salami and Bocconcini Pide Bread Fingers

SERVES 4

SUITABLE FOR GRAZING BOARD

1 large Turkish pide bread loaf
1 x 180 g (6 oz) jar pesto
125 g (4 oz) salami, sliced
250 g (8 oz) jar chargrilled capsicum (peppers), drained well
90 g (3 oz) pitted kalamata olives, halved
90 g (3 oz) semi-dried tomatoes
1 tablespoon capers
1 teaspoon dried oregano leaves
150 g (5 oz) bocconcini cheese
60 g (2 oz) feta, crumbled
salt and freshly ground black pepper
extra-virgin olive oil
baby rocket (arugula) leaves, to serve

Preheat oven to 190°C (375°F) and line a large baking tray with non-stick baking paper.

Cut the pide bread in half lengthways and spread both sides with as much pesto as you like. Arrange the salami slices on top of one half followed by the chargrilled capsicums. Scatter the olives on top, then the tomatoes and capers and sprinkle with the oregano. Tear the bocconcini in half and arrange on top with the crumbled feta, season with a little salt and a good grind of pepper. Drizzle with a little extra olive oil, cover with the other half of the bread and press firmly together.

Place onto the prepared baking tray and bake for 20–25 minutes until crispy and the cheese has melted. Remove from oven and let it rest for about 10–15 minutes before cutting into four pieces and serving on a bed of baby rocket leaves. Cut into fingers if using on a grazing board.

Note: Use your favourite hot or mild salami in this recipe.

Crispy Pita Triangles

MAKES 32 TRIANGLES

SUITABLE FOR GRAZING BOARD

60 ml (2 fl oz) extra-virgin olive oil
2–3 cloves garlic, finely grated
1½ teaspoons sumac spice
1½ teaspoons dukkah spice
½ teaspoon chilli flakes
salt and freshly ground black pepper
4 Lebanese pita breads

Preheat oven to 190°C (375°F) and line two baking trays with baking paper.

Mix together the olive oil, garlic, spices, chilli, salt and pepper. Brush the pita breads liberally with the oil mixture and cut each one into 8 triangles. Place the triangles on the baking tray and bake for about 5–7 minutes, until lightly browned and crispy. Keep an eye on the pitas as they can burn quickly.

They will keep for quite a few days stored in an airtight container.

Note: Sumac is a Mediterranean spice and dukkah a spice blend, usually with nuts and seeds. They are available at most supermarkets and delicatessens.

Foccacia Bread

SERVES 6–8

SUITABLE FOR GRAZING BOARD

- 400 g (14 oz) plain flour
- 2 teaspoons dried yeast
- 2 teaspoons sea salt
- 150 g (5 oz) pitted kalamata olives, sliced
- 1 tablespoon chopped fresh thyme leaves, plus extra to garnish
- 250 ml (8 fl oz) warm water
- 100 ml (3½ fl oz) extra-virgin olive oil
- 1 teaspoon chopped rosemary

Lightly oil a 26 x 33 cm (10 x 13 in) baking dish.

Sift the flour into a bowl and stir in the yeast and salt. Add the olives and thyme leaves and mix to completely coat in the flour mixture.

Slowly pour in the water, alternating with the oil, and mix with your hands to form a soft, pliable dough. If the dough feels dry add a little more water.

Place the dough into the baking dish and with slightly damp hands stretch it out to completely cover the bottom of the dish. Cover with a clean tea towel and let it rise in a warm spot for about 2 hours.

Preheat oven to 190°C (375°F).

When the dough has risen, using your index finger make indentations all over the dough. Brush the bread with a little more olive oil and sprinkle with the rosemary and extra thyme leaves. Place in the oven on a middle shelf and bake for about 20–30 minutes until golden brown and the bread sounds hollow when tapped.

As soon as it comes out of the oven brush the bread with a little more extra-virgin olive oil and sprinkle with a little more sea salt. Cut into fingers or square pieces and serve.

Best served on the same day it is baked.

SALADS

Asparagus with Prosciutto, Dijon Mustard and Parmesan

SERVES 4–6

SUITABLE FOR GRAZING BOARD

12 asparagus spears
dijon mustard
125 g (4 oz) grated parmesan cheese
12 thin slices of prosciutto
extra-virgin olive oil
freshly ground black pepper

Preheat oven to 185°C (350°F) and line a baking tray with non-stick baking paper.

Trim the asparagus and brush the top half with a generous coating of dijon mustard then coat with the parmesan cheese.

Carefully wrap a slice of prosciutto around the top half of each asparagus and place on the baking tray. Brush each one with a little olive oil then bake for about 10–15 minutes until the asparagus is tender and prosciutto crisp.

Serve immediately with a good sprinkle of black pepper.

Kale, Bean, Sun-dried Tomato and Artichoke Salad

SERVES 4–6

VEGAN

6–8 large kale leaves
4 tablespoons extra-virgin olive oil
2 tablespoons red wine vinegar
salt and pepper
1 cup pitted black kalamata olives
150 g (5 oz) chargrilled capsicum (pepper)
125 g (4 oz) sun-dried tomatoes, sliced
280 g (10 oz) jar artichoke hearts, cut into quarters
2 x 400 g (14 oz) cans small butter beans, drained and rinsed
2 tablespoons capers, drained
1–2 red chillies, seeded and chopped
1 small red onion, finely chopped

Thoroughly wash the kale, discard the thick stalks, finely shred the leaves and place in a bowl. Mix the olive oil, vinegar, salt and pepper and pour over the kale. Using your fingers lightly massage the dressing into the kale: this allows the kale to soften and breaks down the fibres. Mix well then leave to stand for about 5–10 minutes.

Halve the olives lengthways and cut the capsicums into strips. Add to the bowl with the tomatoes, artichoke hearts, beans, capers, chilli and onion. Toss well to combine. Taste and adjust the seasoning and dressing according to your taste.

Note: Some people may find the raw kale to be a little sharp on the tongue. If you prefer, before shredding the kale leaves you can blanch them in boiling water for 1–2 minutes, then plunge into ice cold water to stop the cooking process.

Chickpea, Olive and Feta Salad

SERVES 6

VEGETARIAN

2 x 400 g (14 oz) cans chickpeas (garbanzos), rinsed and drained
150 g (5 oz) stuffed green olives
280 g (10 oz) jar chargrilled capsicum (pepper)
60 g (2 oz) baby spinach leaves
1 small red onion, finely chopped
good handful of flat-leaf parsley, roughly chopped
150 g (5 oz) feta cheese, crumbled

Dressing
1 clove garlic, finely grated
juice of 1 lemon
1 teaspoon horseradish cream (optional)
¼ cup extra-virgin olive oil
salt and freshly ground black pepper

Combine the chickpeas with the olives, capsicums, spinach, onion and parsley, and mix well. Whisk together the garlic, lemon juice, horseradish cream (if using), and olive oil, season with salt and pepper and then gently toss the dressing through the salad.

Place salad onto a serving platter and scatter the feta on top. Drizzle a little extra-virgin olive oil over the salad before serving.

Roast Pumpkin, Spinach and Lentil Salad

SERVES 4–6

VEGAN

1 kg (35 oz) butternut pumpkin (squash)
2 x 400 g (14 oz) cans lentils, rinsed and drained
1 medium red onion, finely sliced
100 g (3½ oz) baby spinach leaves
½ cup chopped coriander (cilantro)
zest and juice of 1 lemon
3 tablespoons extra-virgin olive oil
salt and pepper to taste

Preheat oven to 200°C (400°F) and line a large baking tray with non-stick baking paper.

Peel and chop pumpkin into small pieces, drizzle with a little extra-virgin olive oil and bake until cooked and charred along the edges, about 20 minutes. Remove from oven and cool.

When cool, place the pumpkin and lentils into a mixing bowl with all the other ingredients, toss well and transfer to a serving dish.

Prosciutto, Buffalo Mozzarella and Fig Salad

SERVES 4–6

1 tablespoon dijon mustard
1 tablespoon honey
2 tablespoons white or red wine vinegar
⅓ cup extra-virgin olive oil
salt and pepper
3 tablespoons finely chopped chives
3 tablespoons finely chopped mint
100 g (3½ oz) baby rocket (arugula)
300 g (11 oz) small buffalo mozzarella or bocconcini
8 fresh ripe figs
150 g (5 oz) thinly sliced prosciutto

Whisk together the mustard, honey, vinegar, olive oil, salt and pepper. Stir in the chives and mint and set aside.

Arrange the rocket over the bottom of a platter. Tear the buffalo mozzarella into pieces and cut the figs into long quarters then arrange on top of the rocket with the prosciutto slices draped in between. Pour the dressing over the salad making sure that all the ingredients have dressing on them.

Serve with a drizzle of extra-virgin olive oil and freshly ground black pepper.

Legumes and Chilli Salad with Lime and Fresh Coriander

SERVES 6–8

VEGAN

2 x 400 g (14 oz) cans brown lentils
400 g (14 oz) can chickpeas (garbanzos)
400 g (14 oz) can borlotti beans
1 small red onion, finely chopped
4 shallots (scallions/spring onions)
3 long red chillies, sliced
½ bunch fresh coriander (cilantro)
salt
juice of 1–2 limes
4–5 tablespoons extra-virgin olive oil

Drain and rinse the lentils, chickpeas and borlotti beans and place in a bowl with the red onion.

Top and tail the shallots leaving quite a bit of the green part, and finely slice diagonally. Add to the bowl with the chillies (deseeded if you prefer them less hot). Wash the coriander, finely chop the stalks and roughly chop the leaves, add to the salad and season with salt to taste. Add the lime juice and olive oil, taste and adjust the seasoning and toss well.

Place in a serving dish and garnish with extra slices of chilli and coriander leaves.

Grilled Broccoli and Fennel Salad

SERVES 4–6

VEGETARIAN

1 kg (35 oz) broccoli
1 head fennel
extra-virgin olive oil
shaved parmesan cheese

Dressing

100 ml (3½ fl oz) extra-virgin olive oil
3 cloves garlic, sliced
1–2 long red chillies, de-seeded and chopped
2 tablespoons chopped chives
2 tablespoons finely chopped flat-leaf parsley
juice of 1–2 lemons
salt and freshly ground black pepper

Cut the broccoli into florets and peel and slice some of the more tender stems. Cook the broccoli in a large saucepan of salted boiling water for 2 minutes only then drain and place in a bowl of iced water to stop the cooking process. Drain well.

Remove and discard any tough outer leaves from the fennel and cut in half. Remove and discard the tough middle core and slice the fennel.

To make the dressing: Heat the oil over gentle heat until hot but not smoking hot. Remove from the heat and toss in the garlic and chilli, swirling the pan so that the garlic and chilli gently cook and become fragrant. Remove from the pan and cool a little. Stir in the chives, parsley, lemon juice to taste and season with salt and pepper.

Lightly salt the broccoli and fennel and coat with a little extra-virgin olive oil then either grill under a hot grill, or with a griddle pan or barbecue until tender and lightly charred. Place in a bowl and toss through the dressing. Serve with shavings of parmesan cheese scattered on top.

Note: Prawns can be added to this salad. Use large green prawns that have been peeled and de-veined. Coat with a little salt and olive oil and grill with the broccoli and fennel until they are cooked.

Summer Pasta Salad

SERVES 4–8

VEGAN

250 g (9 oz) uncooked small pasta such as shells, alternate Vegan Pasta
400 g (14 oz) broccoli
250 g (9 oz) cauliflower
280 g (10 oz) jar artichoke hearts, drained and halved
¾ cup basil leaves, shredded
½ cup chopped flat-leaf parsley

Dressing

125 ml (4 fl oz) extra-virgin olive oil
4 tablespoons balsamic vinegar
1 tablespoon dijon mustard
salt
freshly ground black pepper
1–2 tablespoons capers (optional)

Cook pasta in salted boiling water until al dente, drain and place into a large bowl.

Cut broccoli and cauliflower into florets and blanch in boiling salted water for a few minutes until cooked but still firm. Remove from heat and plunge into iced water to stop the cooking process and for the broccoli to retain its green colour. Drain well and add to the pasta with the artichoke, basil and parsley.

To make the dressing: mix all ingredients together.

Pour dressing over salad, toss well, and allow to stand for at least 30 minutes before serving.

Note: You can add diced salami or pieces of cooked chicken to this salad.

Potato and Tomato Salad

SERVES 4–6

VEGAN

- 1 kg (35 oz) baby chat potatoes, boiled and halved
- 125 ml (4 fl oz) extra-virgin olive oil
- 2 tablespoons balsamic or red wine vinegar
- salt and freshly ground pepper
- 500 g (18 oz) red grape or cherry tomatoes, halved
- 1 red onion, peeled, halved and thinly sliced
- 125 g (4 oz) pitted kalamata olives
- large handful chopped flat-leaf parsley leaves

You can peel the potatoes if you wish but it's really not necessary. Place potatoes in a bowl while still a little warm. Whisk together the oil, vinegar, salt and pepper and pour over the potatoes and gently toss. Leave to stand until the potatoes are completely cool.

Add the tomatoes, onion, olives and parsley, check and adjust the seasoning and add more dressing if needed.

This salad is best prepared about 2 hours before serving to allow all the flavours to combine. Place salad onto serving platter and serve at room temperature.

Fattoush Salad

SERVES 4

VEGAN

2 Lebanese flatbreads
2 Lebanese cucumbers
250 g (9 oz) cherry tomatoes, halved
1 red onion, finely chopped
4 shallots (scallions/spring onions), sliced
½ large red capsicum (pepper), diced
½ large green capsicum (pepper), diced
4 radishes, sliced
½ cup roughly chopped fresh mint
½ cup roughly chopped flat parsley
½ cup roughly chopped fresh coriander (cilantro)
3 tablespoons lemon juice
4 tablespoons extra-virgin olive oil
2–3 teaspoons sumac
1 teaspoon za'atar
salt
freshly ground black pepper

Toast bread under a hot grill until golden brown, or crisp in a hot oven. When cooled break into small pieces.

Cut cucumbers in four lengthways and dice, place into a large bowl with all the other ingredients including bread and toss well.

You can serve this salad as a side dish or as a main meal.

Note: Sumac and za'atar are seasonings that are widely used in Middle Eastern cooking and can be found at most delicatessens and some supermarkets.

Quinoa Tabouleh

SERVES 6

VEGAN

200 g (7 oz) uncooked quinoa
500 ml (16 fl oz) water
2 firm ripe tomatoes
2–3 cups chopped flat-leaf parsley
1 red onion, finely chopped
4 shallots (scallions/spring onions), sliced
2 Lebanese cucumbers, diced
juice of ½–1 lemon
80 ml (2½ fl oz) extra-virgin olive oil
salt and pepper to taste

Put the quinoa in a fine sieve and rinse under cold running water then drain. Place into a small saucepan with the water, bring to the boil, reduce heat, cover and simmer for 10 minutes or until water fully absorbed. Remove from heat and cool completely.

Slice, de-seed and dice tomatoes and place in a large bowl with the cooled quinoa and all the other salad ingredients. Toss well. Add lemon juice and oil, season with salt and pepper and toss to thoroughly combine. If possible allow to stand for at least half an hour before serving.

Note: Traditionally tabouleh is made out of cracked wheat/bourghul which makes it unsuitable for anyone who has a gluten or wheat intolerance.

Steak and Lentil Salad

SERVES 4

2 x 250 g (9 oz) eye fillet steaks
2 x 400 g (14 oz) cans lentils, drained and rinsed
2 tablespoons dijon grain mustard
3 tablespoons chopped fresh chives
4 shallots (scallions/spring onions), thinly sliced
5 tablespoons extra-virgin olive oil
salt and pepper
500 g (18 oz) grape tomatoes, halved
1 large avocado, peeled and diced
15 pitted kalamata olives, halved
1 tablespoon capers
2 tablespoons chopped coriander (cilantro)
lime juice to taste
salt and pepper
200 g (7 oz) baby rocket (arugula) leaves
handful coriander (cilantro) leaves

Rub steak with a little extra-virgin olive oil, season with salt and pepper and cook on a hot griddle for 3–4 minutes each side. Cover with foil and allow to rest.

While steak is cooking prepare the salad by combining the lentils, mustard, chives, shallots and 2 tablespoons of olive oil, and season with salt and pepper. In another bowl combine tomatoes, avocado, olives, capers, coriander, 3 tablespoons olive oil, lime juice, salt and pepper, and toss well.

Place rocket leaves on the bottom of a large serving platter, top with the lentils then the tomato mixture. Thinly slice steak and place on top of salad, garnish with some coriander leaves and serve.

Salade Niçoise

SERVES 4–6

300 g (11 oz) fresh green beans
400 g (14 oz) can tuna, drained and flaked into large chunks
10–12 baby chat potatoes, boiled and halved or quartered
2 firm ripe tomatoes cut into wedges
1 medium red onion, halved and finely sliced
120 g (4 oz) pitted kalamata olives
2 Lebanese cucumbers, cubed
3 hard boiled eggs, peeled and quartered
chopped flat-leaf parsley

Dressing

4 anchovy fillets, chopped (optional)
125 ml (4 fl oz) extra-virgin olive oil
2–3 tablespoons balsamic vinegar
1 clove garlic, very finely grated
salt and freshly ground black pepper

Top and tail beans and cut into 5 cm (2 in) pieces. Blanch in salted boiling water until the beans are just tender but still have a bit of crunch in them. Rinse in icy cold water to stop the cooking process and drain well.

To make the dressing: Whisk all the ingredients together.

Place the beans, tuna, potatoes, tomatoes, onion, olives and cucumber into a large bowl and toss lightly with some of the dressing. Transfer the salad to a serving platter, arrange the eggs over the salad, sprinkle with parsley and pour over the remaining dressing. Serve as a main meal or side salad.

Note: This is a meal on its own and you really don't need anything else served with it. The number of servings you get really depends on your guests' appetite.

Artichoke, Olive and Broccoli Pasta Salad

SERVES 6

VEGAN

200 g (7 oz) small pasta such as shells, alternate Vegan Pasta
500 g (18 oz) broccoli, cut into florets
250 g (9 oz) small grape tomatoes
125 g (4 oz) pitted kalamata olives
280 g (10 oz) jar of artichokes, drained and quartered
2 tablespoons capers (optional)
4 shallots (scallions/spring onions), sliced

Dressing

1 small clove garlic, finely grated
100 ml (3½ fl oz) extra-virgin olive oil
1 tablespoon dijon mustard
1 tablespoon honey
2 tablespoons red wine vinegar
salt and freshly ground black pepper

Cook the pasta in salted boiling water until al dente, drain well and rinse under cold running water to stop the cooking process and drain again.

Bring a large saucepan of salted water to the boil, add the broccoli and cook for 2–3 minutes until just tender but still a little firm. Drain and place in a bowl of iced water to stop the cooking process and for the broccoli to retain that vibrant green colour. When completely cooled drain well and place into a large bowl with the pasta, tomatoes, olives, artichokes, capers and shallots. Gently toss to combine.

To make the dressing: Whisk all the ingredients together.

Pour dressing over the salad and toss. Taste and adjust the seasoning.

The salad is best if prepared at least 2–3 hours in advance to allow all the flavours to combine and for the pasta and broccoli to absorb the dressing.

Borlotti Bean, Rocket and Tomato Salad

SERVES 4–6

VEGAN

2 x 400 g (14 oz) cans borlotti beans, rinsed and drained
2 celery stalks, diced
250 g (9 oz) grape or cherry tomatoes, left whole or halved
100 g (3½ oz) baby rocket (arugula)
1 red onion, finely chopped
2 cloves garlic, finely grated
2 tablespoons capers
12 basil leaves, torn into small pieces
2 tablespoons chopped chives
1–2 tablespoons lemon juice
4 tablespoons extra-virgin olive oil
1½ tablespoons red wine vinegar
salt and freshly ground pepper

Place the beans in a bowl with the celery including some of the young tender leaves, tomatoes, rocket, onion, garlic, capers, basil and chives.

Whisk together the lemon juice, oil and vinegar and season with salt and pepper. Adjust the amount of oil, lemon and vinegar to taste then pour over the salad. Toss well and serve.

Note: This salad can be enjoyed as a main meal or a side salad. Great for a barbecue.

Pasta and Kale Salad

SERVES 6–8

VEGAN

250 g (9 oz) small pasta of your choice, alternate Vegan Pasta
6 large stalks of cavolo nero (Tuscan) kale
250 g (9 oz) jar artichoke hearts, drained
250 g (9 oz) jar chargrilled capsicum (pepper), drained
90 g (3 oz) semi-dried tomatoes
1 cup pitted kalamata olives
1 tablespoon capers, drained (optional)
4–6 shallots (scallions/spring onions), finely sliced
½ cup finely chopped flat-leaf parsley
4–5 tablespoons extra-virgin olive oil
1–2 tablespoons balsamic vinegar
salt and freshly ground black pepper

Cook pasta in salted boiling water until al dente, drain and rinse under cold running water to stop cooking process. Drain again and set aside.

Thoroughly wash the kale, remove and discard the entire stalk and chop the leaves into fine strips. Use a salad spinner or wrap in a clean kitchen towel to remove any excess moisture and dry.

Cut the artichoke hearts into quarters and slice the capsicums and tomatoes into strips.

Place the pasta, kale, artichokes, capsicums, sun-dried tomatoes and olives into a large bowl. Add the capers, shallots and parsley and toss well.

Whisk together the oil, vinegar, salt and pepper. Pour the dressing over the salad and toss well. Check and adjust the seasoning and the amount of dressing.

Leave the salad to stand for about 30 minutes for all the flavours to combine before serving on a serving platter.

A great salad to feed a crowd on any occasion. A real taste of the Mediterranean in a bowl and a salad that would complement any other food on the table.

PASTA & RICE

Creamy Polenta

SERVES 2–4

1 litre (32 fl oz) chicken stock
150 g (5 oz) fine polenta/cornmeal
2 tablespoons butter
90 g (3 oz) grated parmesan cheese
salt to taste

Bring the stock to the boil in a medium saucepan then slowly pour in the polenta, stirring continuously with a whisk. Keep whisking over medium heat until the polenta starts to thicken, about 3–5 minutes. Reduce the heat to low and continue to cook for 5–8 minutes until the polenta is thick, stirring every now and then with a wooden spoon.

At this stage, although thick, the polenta should still be quite soft. Stir in the butter and parmesan until well combined, cook for another minute or so. Taste and adjust the seasoning if needed.

Serve immediately garnished with a little extra parmesan cheese.

Note: Polenta is real comfort food and great as a substitute for mashed potatoes. Polenta should be soft and creamy, almost porridgy. As it cools polenta sets very quickly to hard. If there are any leftovers, place cold polenta back into a saucepan, add hot water or milk a little at a time and stir over low heat until it returns to a soft consistency.

Lentil Pilaf

SERVES 4–6

VEGAN

1 large leek
4 tablespoons extra-virgin olive oil
4 cloves garlic, finely chopped
1 teaspoon cumin seed
1 tablespoon ground cumin
1 teaspoon ground turmeric
1 teaspoon ground coriander
2–3 red chillies, de-seeded and sliced (optional)
2 x 400 g (14 oz) cans brown lentils, rinsed and drained
350 g (12 oz) basmati rice
750 ml (24 fl oz) hot water
salt to taste
500 g (18 oz) frozen beans
lemon or lime juice

Wash the leek really well to remove all dirt and grit that may be lodged between the leaves and slice finely.

Heat the oil in a large saucepan or frying pan over medium heat and cook the leek until soft. Add the garlic and cumin seed and cook for about 30 seconds, making sure the garlic does not burn. Stir in the ground cumin, turmeric, coriander and chilli and cook until fragrant, about 30 seconds. Add the lentils, rice and water, season with salt to taste, cover, reduce the heat and simmer on low for about 10 minutes. Stir in the frozen beans and cook for a further 5–8 minutes until the rice and beans are cooked. Turn off the heat and allow to rest for 5–10 minutes before serving with a squeeze of lemon or lime juice.

Pancetta and Bocconcini Pasta Bake

SERVES 6–8

450 g (16 oz) penne pasta
2 tablespoons olive oil
1 onion, finely chopped
6 shallots (scallions/spring onions), sliced
250 g (9 oz) thickly sliced pancetta, chopped
3 cloves garlic, finely chopped
2 tablespoons tomato paste
400 g (14 oz) can diced tomatoes
½–1 teaspoon chilli flakes
salt
good handful fresh basil, shredded
300 g (11 oz) bocconcini cheese
4 tablespoons grated parmesan cheese

Cook pasta in a large pot of salted boiling water until al dente and drain.

Preheat oven to 190°C (375°F).

While the pasta is cooking, heat the oil in a large frying pan over medium heat and sauté onion and shallots until golden. Add the pancetta and cook for 3–4 minutes until it starts to crisp up then stir in the garlic and cook for another 30 seconds until fragrant. Stir in the tomato paste and cook for 1 minute then add the tomatoes and chilli. Season with salt if necessary. Stir in the basil leaves and simmer on low heat for approximately 5 minutes.

Add the pasta to the sauce and mix thoroughly until well combined then spoon into a baking dish. Tear bocconcini into pieces and place on top of the pasta, sprinkle parmesan all over and bake for 15–20 minutes until golden and the bocconcini has melted.

Quick Tomato, Herb and Chilli Pasta Sauce

SERVES 4

VEGAN

500 g (18 oz) pasta
3–4 tablespoons extra-virgin olive oil
6 large cloves garlic, finely sliced
2 fresh tomatoes, chopped
large handful basil leaves, roughly chopped
small handful flat-leaf parsley, roughly chopped
2–3 chillies, sliced
salt
freshly ground black pepper
grated parmesan cheese or vegan substitute

Cook your favourite pasta in a large pot of salted boiling water until al dente.

While the water is coming to the boil, heat the oil in a large frying pan over medium heat and sauté the garlic until it just starts to change colour, being careful not to burn. Stir in the tomatoes, herbs and chillies and cook until the tomatoes just start to break down. Season with salt and pepper.

Drain the pasta and add it to the sauce with a little of the pasta water. Mix well and serve with lots of grated parmesan cheese and a drizzle of extra-virgin oil.

Penne with Yoghurt and Caramelised Onions

SERVES 2–3

125 ml (4 fl oz) extra-virgin olive oil
2 large onions, halved and thinly sliced
2 cloves garlic, finely chopped
250 g (9 oz) penne pasta
300 g (11 oz) Greek yoghurt
125 g (4 oz) grated pecorino cheese
salt and freshly ground black pepper

Heat oil in a large deep frying pan over high heat and cook the onion until crisp and dark brown. They must be well browned and caramelised, almost to the point of getting burnt. Add the garlic and cook until fragrant. When cooked, remove some of the onions and set aside to use as garnish.

While the onions are caramelising, cook the penne in salted boiling water, drain and reserve some of the cooking water.

Add drained pasta to the onions, stir, then add the yoghurt, half the cheese, and season with salt and lots of pepper. Mix until well combined. Serve immediately with the remaining cheese sprinkled on top and garnished with the remaining onions.

Note: If you feel the pasta is heavy as the yoghurt is too thick you can use some of the pasta water to loosen the sauce. You can use low-fat yoghurt if you prefer.

Pasta with Chorizo Sausage, Olives and Sun-Dried Tomatoes

SERVES 4

500 g (18 oz) pasta such as penne
3 tablespoons olive oil
3 chorizo sausages, halved then sliced
4 cloves garlic, chopped
½ teaspoon chilli flakes (optional)
150 g (5 oz) pitted black olives
150 g (5 oz) sun-dried or semi-dried tomatoes
2 tablespoons capers (optional)
freshly ground black pepper
good handful of flat-leaf parsley, chopped
grated parmesan cheese

Cook pasta in a large pot of salted boiling water until al dente.

While the pasta is cooking, heat the oil in a large frying pan over medium–high heat, add the chorizo and sauté until it starts to change colour. Stir in the garlic and chilli and cook for 30 seconds then add the olives, sun-dried tomatoes, capers, pepper and parsley and cook for another 1–2 minutes.

Add the cooked and drained pasta to the pan with a little of the pasta water and toss well to combine. Stir in the grated parmesan cheese and serve with an extra sprinkling of parmesan cheese.

Spaghetti with Mushrooms and Garlic

SERVES 4

VEGAN

500 g (18 oz) spaghetti
3–4 tablespoons extra-virgin olive oil
500 g (18 oz) mushrooms, thinly sliced
4–5 cloves garlic, finely chopped
¾ cup chopped flat-leaf parsley
salt and freshly ground pepper
grated parmesan or pecorino cheese (or Vegan substutite)

Cook pasta in lots of salted boiling water until al dente, drain and reserve some of the cooking water.

While the pasta is cooking, heat the oil in a large deep frying pan over medium–high heat, add the mushrooms and cook until they have softened and collapsed. Stir in the garlic and parsley and cook for 1–2 minutes. Season with salt and lots of freshly ground pepper.

Stir in the spaghetti and add a little of the cooking water, if required. Serve with a good sprinkling of grated parmesan or pecorino cheese.

Note: You can add some chilli to this dish and baby rocket or spinach leaves can be stirred through at the last stage of cooking.

Porcini Mushroom Risotto

SERVES 4

40 g (1½ oz) dried porcini mushrooms
1.5 litres (50 fl oz) hot chicken stock
3 tablespoons extra-virgin olive oil
375 g (13 oz) white mushrooms, thinly sliced
1 heaped tablespoon butter
1 medium brown onion, finely chopped
450 g (16 oz) arborio rice
3–4 cloves garlic, finely chopped
125 ml (4 fl oz) white wine
1–2 tablespoons butter
3–4 tablespoons grated parmesan cheese
3 tablespoons flat-leaf parsley, chopped
salt and pepper

Put the porcini mushrooms in a bowl, cover with boiling water and soak for about 10 minutes until the mushrooms rehydrate and soften. Drain, reserving the liquid, and set aside.

Place the stock in a saucepan, bring to a simmer and leave to simmer on a very low heat.

Heat 2 tablespoons of olive oil in a large saucepan over medium–high heat. Add the porcini and white mushrooms and sauté until soft and just starting to take on some colour. Remove from the pan and set aside.

Heat the remaining oil and butter over medium heat in the same pan and sauté the onion until soft and translucent. Stir in the rice and cook for 1–2 minutes until the rice is all coated and becoming opaque then stir in the garlic and cook for about 30 seconds until fragrant. Add the wine and stir until it is absorbed then start to add the hot stock and the soaking liquid from the porcini mushrooms a ladleful or two at a time. Allow each ladleful to be fully absorbed before adding the next. Stir the rice regularly while doing this and continue to do so until three-quarters of the stock is used up and the rice is tender but not completely cooked, approximately 30 minutes. Stir in the mushrooms and continue adding remaining stock and stirring for another 8–10 minutes until the rice is soft. Stir in the extra butter, parmesan cheese and parsley. Taste and season if needed and serve immediately.

Garlic and Chilli Prawn Linguine

SERVES 1

60 ml (2 fl oz) extra-virgin olive oil
4 cloves garlic, grated
3 bullseye chillies, finely chopped
6 extra-large green king prawns, peeled and de-veined
180 g (6 oz) dry linguine pasta
125 g (4 oz) cherry tomatoes, halved
good handful of flat-leaf parsley, finely chopped, plus extra to garnish
salt to taste
90 g (3 oz) baby spinach
juice of ½ a lemon
shaved parmesan cheese (optional)

Put oil, garlic, and chillies in a bowl and mix to make a marinade. Add the peeled prawns and coat well, cover and set aside in the fridge to marinate for 1 hour.

Bring a large pot of water to the boil, add the pasta and cook until al dente. Drain and rinse under cold water until cool. This will stop the cooking process and keep it al dente. Set aside.

Heat a frying pan on a medium–high heat and add the prawns to the pan with the marinade. Cook prawns for approximately 2–3 minutes. The prawns will change colour starting from the outside and the inner flesh will slowly change colour the longer they are cooked.

Add the cherry tomatoes, parsley and salt to the pan and toss for 30 seconds. Add the baby spinach and lemon juice and toss for another 30 seconds until the spinach starts to wilt. Add the cooked linguine and toss together before serving.

Garnish with the extra parsley and shaved parmesan cheese.

Note: This recipe was given to me by my friend Christopher Grill. It has become his signature dish and is absolutely delicious. A must to make, you will love it!

Spaghettini alle vongole

SERVES 4

1 kg (35 oz) fresh clams (vongole)
400 g (14 oz) spaghettini
2–3 tablespoons extra-virgin olive oil
4–6 cloves garlic, thinly sliced
½–1 teaspoon chilli flakes
165 ml (5½ fl oz) white wine
good handful finely chopped flat-leaf parsley

Note: Some clams can be quite salty, which makes the brine salty. It's best to under salt the water when cooking the pasta and then add more salt to the dish when cooked, if necessary.

Buy clams that have been purged of any sand. If not then cover in cold water and leave to stand for about an hour. Discard any clams that are open or have broken shells.

Bring a large pot of salted water to the boil, add the pasta and cook for 3 minutes only. Drain but reserve the pasta water.

While the water is coming to the boil, heat the oil in a large, deep frying pan/skillet over medium heat until just hot. Add the garlic and sauté until it just starts to change colour, being careful not to burn.

Stir in as much chilli as you would like and cook for a few seconds only. Pour in the wine, cook for about 2 minutes until the alcohol evaporates then add the clams and give the pan a good swirl. Cover with a tight-fitting lid and cook until all the clams open and have released their brine. Give the pan a good toss with the lid on every now and then.

Remove the clams from the pan as they open and set aside.

Add the partially cooked pasta and some of the pasta water (about ½–1 cup) to the pan with the clam brine. Keep tossing or stirring the pasta so that it absorbs the clam brine and continues to cook in the brine for 3–4 minutes. Return the clams to the pan, add the parsley, toss with the pasta and continue to cook for 1–2 minutes until heated through. If you think the pan is too dry add a little more pasta water.

Taste and adjust the seasoning and serve with a drizzle of extra-virgin olive oil.

Spaghetti with Lemon

SERVES 2–4

juice of 1–2 lemons
zest of 1 lemon
165 ml (5½ fl oz) extra-virgin olive oil
3–4 tablespoons grated parmesan cheese
2–3 tablespoons fresh flat-leaf parsley
salt (optional)
generous amount of freshly ground black pepper
300 g (11 oz) thin spaghettini
very thin slices of lemon, to garnish
shaved parmesan cheese

Whisk together the lemon juice, zest and olive oil in a large bowl. Mix in the parmesan, parsley, salt and pepper and set aside.

Cook the spaghetti in lots of salted boiling water until al dente and reserve a little of the cooking water. Drain the spaghetti, toss in the lemon sauce and a little of the cooking water and serve immediately with lemon slices and shavings of parmesan cheese.

Note: This is a deliciously light dish that would be perfect as a light starter or for lunch.

Mushroom and Prosciutto Risotto

SERVES 3–4

1.25 litres (40 fl oz) hot chicken stock
4 tablespoons extra-virgin olive oil
4 shallots (scallions/spring onions), chopped
2 cloves garlic, finely chopped
300 g (11 oz) mushrooms, sliced
150 g (5 oz) prosciutto, sliced
2 tablespoons chopped flat-leaf parsley
1 medium onion, finely chopped
350 g (12 oz) arborio rice
125 ml (4 fl oz) white wine
salt and pepper
1–2 tablespoons butter
3 tablespoons grated parmesan cheese

Place the stock in a saucepan, bring to a simmer and leave to simmer on a very low heat.

Heat 2 tablespoons of the olive oil in a frying pan over medium heat and sauté the shallots until golden then stir in the garlic and cook for another minute until fragrant. Add the mushrooms and cook until soft. Add the prosciutto and cook for 1 minute. Stir in the parsley, remove from the heat and set aside.

Heat the remaining olive oil in a heavy based saucepan over medium heat and sauté the onion until soft. Stir in the rice and cook for 1–2 minutes until it starts to change colour and becomes opaque. Add the wine and stir until it is absorbed. Season with salt and pepper, then add the hot stock a ladleful or two at a time, allowing each to be fully absorbed before adding the next. Stir the rice constantly while doing this and continue to do so until all the stock is used up and the rice is cooked and soft, approximately 25–30 minutes. Stir in the mushrooms and prosciutto. Add the butter and parmesan cheese, give the risotto a good stir and serve immediately.

Note: I love my risotto to be really soft and gooey, almost porridgy, so I tend to cook it for the full 30 minutes, if not more, and sometimes I also add extra stock. You may need to vary the cooking time and amount of stock to suit your taste.

Rice with Turmeric, Leek and Lentils

SERVES 4–6

VEGAN

3 tablespoons extra-virgin olive oil
2 leeks, washed and sliced
3 cloves garlic, chopped
3–4 tablespoons freshly grated turmeric
450 g (16 oz) basmati rice, rinsed
2 x 400 g (14 oz) cans lentils, rinsed and drained
875 ml (28 fl oz) hot vegetable stock
salt and pepper
lemon juice, to serve

Heat the oil in a large saucepan over medium–high heat and sauté the leek until tender. Stir in the garlic and turmeric and cook for 2–3 minutes. Stir in the rice and cook for a couple of minutes until it's thoroughly coated. Add the lentils and season with salt and pepper. Pour in the stock and bring to the boil, reduce the heat and simmer for about 20 minutes until the rice is cooked and all the liquid has been absorbed.

Serve with a good squeeze of lemon juice.

Note: Fresh turmeric is available at many greengrocers and supermarkets. It is usually the size of an index finger and looks like a small, shrivelled up carrot. It's a good idea to wear gloves when peeling and grating turmeric as it can discolour your fingers.

MEAT

Greek Lamb Cutlets

SERVES 4–6

SUITABLE FOR GRAZING BOARD

12 lamb cutlets or lamb loin chops
3–4 cloves garlic, finely chopped
1 tablespoon dried oregano leaves
juice of 1 lemon
2 tablespoons olive oil
salt and pepper
lemon wedges for serving

Place lamb in a deep dish and add garlic, oregano, lemon juice, olive oil, salt and pepper. Mix well to thoroughly coat the lamb with the marinade. Cover and place in the fridge to marinate for at least 2 hours.

Heat a griddle pan or grill until hot and cook the lamb for about 2–3 minutes only on each side until browned on the outside and still slightly pink on the inside.

Serve with lemon wedges and or tzatziki dip (page 34).

Note: These lamb chops are always a huge hit and there are never any leftovers. They go so well with the tzatziki dip. These are also great served with caramelised lemons and garlic. Simply heat some oil in a frying pan and cook whole unpeeled cloves of garlic and wedges of lemon until caramelised.

Baked Shoulder of Lamb with Risoni

SERVES 4–6

- 1 x 2 kg (4 lb 6 oz) lamb shoulder (with bone)
- 2 cloves garlic, peeled and halved
- 2 tablespoons extra-virgin olive oil
- 2 medium onions, grated
- 3–4 cloves garlic, finely chopped
- 1 x 700 g (26½ oz) bottle passata sauce
- 2 teaspoons ground cinnamon
- 250 ml (9 fl oz) water
- salt and freshly ground black pepper
- 500 g (18 oz) risoni pasta
- 750 ml (24 fl oz) boiling water, extra
- grated parmesan cheese

Preheat oven to 180°C (350°F).

Make four incisions in the lamb, insert a garlic half into each one and place onto a large baking pan.

Mix together the oil, onion, garlic, passata, cinnamon and water and season with salt and pepper. Pour the tomato mixture over the lamb and cover with a tight lid or a double layer of foil.

Bake for 2½ hours then remove the cover, increase oven temperature to 200°C (400°F) and continue baking for another 45–60 minutes until the lamb is tender and browned. Baste the lamb with the juices occasionally.

Remove the lamb from the pan, set aside and keep warm. Skim off any fat that has risen to the surface of the pan then stir in the risoni and pour in the boiling water, return to the oven and bake for 30–45 minutes stirring regularly until the risoni is cooked and the liquid is absorbed. If risoni dries out add a little extra water.

Remove from the oven, cover and allow to rest for 10–15 minutes for the liquid to be completely absorbed before serving with the lamb, lots of parmesan cheese and a beautiful salad. The lamb can either be sliced or pulled off the bone.

Beef Pot Roast in Red Wine

SERVES 4–6

1½ kg (3 lb 5 oz) beef roast in one piece
2–3 cloves garlic, peeled and left whole
60 ml (2 fl oz) extra-virgin olive oil
1 large onion, finely chopped
3 cloves garlic, finely chopped
250 ml (8 fl oz) red wine
500 ml (16 fl oz) water
2 bay leaves
salt and freshly ground black pepper

Make 2–3 incisions in the beef and insert a whole clove of garlic in each incision.

Heat the oil in a large saucepan on high heat and brown the meat all over. Add the onion and the garlic and cook until the onion is soft and slightly browned. Pour in the wine and cook for 2–3 minutes until the alcohol evaporates then add the water and bay leaves, season with salt and pepper. Bring to the boil, reduce the heat to the lowest, cover with a lid leaving it slightly ajar and simmer for 2–2½ hours until the meat is tender and the liquid in the pan has reduced by about a half.

Serve the beef with the sauce spooned over or if you prefer you can thicken the sauce by stirring in some cornflour which has been mixed with some cold water and cook until thickened.

Note: My mother used to peel and roast small (chat) potatoes then add them to the pot for about 10 minutes before serving. This allows the potatoes to absorb some of the delicious liquid.

Stuffed Tomatoes with Mince and Rice

SERVES 4–6

1.5–2 kg (3–4 lb) medium-sized tomatoes
salt
4–6 tablespoons extra-virgin olive oil
500 g (18 oz) lean minced steak
2 cloves garlic, grated
2 medium onions, grated
2 tablespoons tomato paste
5 tablespoons chopped flat-leaf parsley
125 g (4 oz) long grain rice
freshly ground black pepper
165 ml (5½ fl oz) water
30 g (1 oz) packaged breadcrumbs
2 tablespoons grated parmesan cheese

Note: Capsicums (peppers) and eggplants (aubergines) can be filled the same way. Remove the seeds from the capsicums and the pulp from the eggplant before filling with the meat mixture. Use either chopped canned tomatoes or grated fresh tomatoes in the stuffing. A combination of stuffed tomatoes, capsicum and eggplant is quite delicious.

Slice the top off each tomato, scoop out the pulp, finely chop and reserve. Rub the inside of each tomato with a little salt, turn upside down and stand for 10 minutes.

Heat 2–3 tablespoons of oil in a large frying pan over medium–high and brown the mince, garlic and onion. Mix in about one cup of the tomato pulp, tomato paste, 4 tablespoons of parsley, rice, salt and pepper. Add the water and cook on low heat for 15–20 minutes or until most of the liquid has evaporated. Allow to cool. Preheat oven to 180°C (350°F).

Fill each tomato with the meat mixture. Combine the breadcrumbs, cheese and the remaining parsley. Top the tomatoes with some of the cheese mixture and place in a large baking dish. Mix any remaining tomato pulp with a cup of water and the remaining 2–3 tablespoons of oil, pour into the baking dish and bake for 40–50 minutes. Baste with juices and add a little extra water during cooking if needed.

Chorizo Sausage Antipasto

SERVES 4

SUITABLE FOR GRAZING BOARD

1 teaspoon olive oil
3 chorizo sausages, thickly sliced
4 cloves garlic, sliced
120 g (4 oz) pitted kalamata olives
250 g (9 oz) chargrilled capsicum (pepper), cut into strips
150 g (5 oz) sun-dried tomatoes
2 tablespoons capers
½ cup chopped flat-leaf parsley leaves
freshly ground pepper

Heat the oil in a large non-stick frying pan and cook the chorizo until lightly browned. Stir in the garlic and cook for about 1 minute until fragrant then add the olives, capsicum, sun-dried tomatoes and capers. Give the pan a good toss and cook for another 1–2 minutes. Add the parsley and a good grind of pepper, toss again and serve.

Meat Loaf

SERVES 6

1 kg (35 oz) finely ground beef mince
1 onion, finely grated
3 cloves garlic, grated
2 large eggs
4 tablespoons finely chopped flat-leaf parsley
35 g (1½ oz) dried breadcrumbs
2 teaspoons dried oregano leaves
1 tablespoon extra-virgin olive oil
salt and pepper
extra breadcrumbs for coating

Filling
4 tablespoons finely chopped flat-leaf parsley
45 g (1½ oz) shaved parmesan cheese
75 g (2½ oz) pitted kalamata olives, halved lengthways
4–5 hardboiled eggs, shelled
extra-virgin olive oil

Preheat oven to 200°C (400°F) and line a 30 x 13 x 8 cm (12 x 5 x 3 in) loaf tin with baking paper, making sure the paper overhangs the sides to make it easier to lift the meatloaf out of the tin.

Place the mince, onion, garlic, eggs, parsley, breadcrumbs, oregano, oil and salt and pepper in a large bowl and mix together until well combined. Place the mince mixture onto a large sheet of baking paper that has been dusted with breadcrumbs and shape into a rectangle. Place the filling into the centre of the mince by firstly sprinkling the parsley, cheese and then the olives over the meat, place the whole eggs in a row over the top then carefully lift the sides of the mince over the top of the egg to fully enclose the filling in the centre of the meat loaf. Cover the entire meatloaf with the extra breadcrumbs.

Carefully lift into the prepared tin, sprinkle with a little olive oil and bake for 75–90 minutes until the meatloaf is cooked and browned on top.

Allow to rest in the tin for a good 20 minutes before lifting out and slicing. Serve with Greek baked potatoes and a salad.

Liver with Rosemary

SERVES 4

500 g (18 oz) calves liver, finely sliced
flour for dusting
125 ml (4 fl oz) extra-virgin olive oil
2 cloves garlic, sliced
1½ tablespoons chopped fresh rosemary
3 tablespoons brown or red wine vinegar
salt and pepper to taste

Lightly dust the slices of liver with flour until coated all over.

Heat the oil in a large frying pan over medium heat and gently fry the liver for about 3 minutes each side until cooked. Remove from the pan and keep warm. Add the garlic and rosemary to the pan and cook for about 30 seconds until fragrant and the garlic just starts to change colour, being careful not to burn.

Take the pan off the heat, hold it away from you, preferably over the sink, and pour in the vinegar. The vinegar will cause the oil to splatter. Return the pan to the heat, add the liver and cook for 1–2 minutes, basting the liver with the pan juices.

Season with salt and pepper to taste and serve with mashed potato.

Lamb Souvlakia

SERVES 4–6

SUITABLE FOR GRAZING BOARD

1 kg (35 oz) cubed lamb
3–4 cloves garlic, finely chopped
2 tablespoons dried oregano leaves
1 tablespoon chopped fresh thyme
3 tablespoons olive oil
juice of 1–2 lemons
salt and freshly ground black pepper
1 capsicum (pepper), cut into chunks
1 onion, peeled, quartered and cut into chunks
cherry tomatoes (optional)
wooden skewers

Place lamb in a bowl with the garlic, oregano, thyme, olive oil, lemon juice, salt and pepper. Mix well to coat the lamb, cover and refrigerate for at least 3–4 hours.

Soak the skewers in cold water for at least half an hour before use. Thread the lamb onto the skewers alternatively with the capsicum, onion and tomato if using.

Grill the souvlaki under a preheated grill, or on a barbecue or griddle pan for 3–4 minutes each side until cooked and browned.

Note: The best cut of lamb to use for this dish is a deboned leg or fillets. The fillets will take less marinating and cooking time. The number of lemons used depends on your personal taste and how juicy the lemons are. You can either have souvlakia with just the lamb or threaded with the vegetables.

Kofta Kebabs

MAKES 12–15

SUITABLE FOR GRAZING BOARD

750 g (27 oz) beef or lamb mince
1 red onion, finely chopped
3 large cloves garlic, grated
3 tablespoons chopped fresh coriander (cilantro)
3 tablespoons chopped fresh flat-leaf parsley
1½ teaspoons ground cumin
1 teaspoon ground coriander
1 teaspoon ground allspice
½–1 teaspoon chilli flakes (optional)
salt and freshly ground black pepper
skewers
olive oil

Place all of the ingredients except the olive oil into a large bowl and mix until thoroughly combined.

Moisten hands with water and take about 2–3 tablespoons of the mince mixture and shape into long sausage shapes around the skewers. Brush each kebab with a little olive oil and grill under a preheated grill, or on a griddle pan or barbecue for a few minutes each side until browned and cooked.

Serve with quinoa tabouleh (page 69), tzatziki (page 34), and/or baba ganoush (page 33).

Note: If using wooden skewers soak in cold water for half an hour before using.

Osso Bucco

SERVES 4

flour
salt and pepper
4 veal osso bucco pieces
2 tablespoons extra-virgin olive oil
1 onion finely chopped
375 ml (13 fl oz) white wine
2 tablespoons tomato paste
250 ml (8 fl oz) water
2 cloves garlic, finely chopped
1 tablespoon lemon juice
2 anchovy fillets, very finely chopped
2 tablespoons finely chopped flat-leaf parsley
salt and freshly ground black pepper
1 tablespoon butter
80 ml (2½ fl oz) beef stock

Garnish

2–3 tablespoons finely chopped flat-leaf parsley
2 cloves garlic, very finely chopped
zest of 1 lemon

Season flour with salt and pepper then dust the veal pieces with the flour.

Heat oil in a large deep frying pan or saucepan over medium–high heat and cook the veal until browned on both sides. Add the onion and cook until soft and golden. Stir in the wine and cook until it has evaporated. Stir in the tomato paste and cook for about a minute then add the water, cover and simmer on low heat for 60–75 minutes or until the veal is tender. Stir in the garlic, lemon juice, anchovies and parsley and simmer for another 20 minutes.

Remove the veal from the pan and cover with foil to keep warm. Combine the garnish ingredients. Add the butter, stock and garnish to the pan and cook for about 2 minutes. Return the veal to the pan, coat with the sauce and serve sprinkled with a little extra finely chopped parsley.

Serve with blanched beans or other green vegetable.

Eggplant (Aubergine) Moussaka

SERVES 6–8

2 kg (4½ lb) eggplant (aubergine), (about 2–3 large)

Meat Sauce

90 ml (3 fl oz) extra-virgin olive oil
2 large onions, finely chopped
1 kg (2 lb 4 oz) beef mince
3 cloves garlic, minced
3 tablespoons tomato paste
500 g (18 oz) canned diced tomatoes
1 teaspoon cinnamon
180 ml (6 fl oz) water
salt and pepper

Cream sauce

90 g (3 oz) butter
6 tablespoons flour
1 litre (32 fl oz) milk
3 eggs, lightly beaten
90 g (3 oz) parmesan or kefalotiri cheese, grated
salt and pepper

Preheat oven to 200°C (400°F).

Slice the eggplant into rounds 1 cm (½ in) thick. Line two baking trays with non-stick paper and place the eggplant slices in a single layer on the prepared trays. Drizzle with a little olive oil and bake for approximately 30 minutes until browned, turning once.

To prepare the meat sauce:
Heat the oil in a large pan over medium–high heat and sauté the onion until golden. Add the mince and cook until well browned, breaking up any lumps as you go. Stir in the garlic, cook until fragrant then add the tomato paste and cook for about a minute. Add the tomatoes, cinnamon and water, season with salt and pepper and simmer on low heat for 30–40 minutes until the sauce thickens.

To prepare the cream sauce:
Melt the butter in a saucepan, remove from the heat and add the flour, stirring to make a smooth paste. Return the pan to a medium heat and slowly add the milk, stirring constantly until the sauce begins to bubble and thicken. Cook for about 1 minute, Once thickened, remove from the heat and allow to cool slightly. Add the eggs a little at a time, stirring constantly and quickly. Stir in the cheese, salt and pepper and mix well. Cook for a further 1–2 minutes until the mixture bubbles and is thick.

Note: Thin slices of uncooked potato can be substituted for the eggplant. Follow the rest of the method above and vary the baking time of the moussaka to ensure the potatoes are cooked through completely (cook for around 15 minutes longer).

The meat sauce can be made in advance and either frozen or kept in the fridge for a few days before assembling the dish.

To assemble the moussaka:

Spread a thin layer of cream sauce over the bottom of a large baking dish 33 x 23 x 5 cm (13 x 9 x 2 in). Place half of eggplant slices over the cream sauce and top with meat sauce. Place the remainder of the eggplant slices over the meat.

Spread the remaining cream sauce over the eggplant and sprinkle with extra cheese and cinnamon.

Bake in a preheated 180°C (350°F) oven for about one hour until browned on top.

Allow to rest for at least 20 minutes before serving.

Moussaka always tastes better the day after making it.

Slow Cooked Lamb

SERVES 6

12 cloves garlic
2.5–3 kg (6 lb 10 oz) leg of lamb
2 tablespoons extra-virgin olive oil
juice of 1½–2 lemons
1 tablespoon sweet paprika
2 tablespoons dried oregano leaves
1 teaspoon dried thyme
salt and freshly ground pepper
500 ml (16 fl oz) water
6 large potatoes quartered

Note: The amount of lemon used is up to you. I always use at least two, depending on how juicy they are. You will definitely need the juice of at least one very juicy lemon.

You can substitute the leg of lamb for a shoulder of lamb; you will need to vary the cooking time to approximately just over half the time.

Preheat the oven to 230°C (450°F).

Peel half the garlic cloves and slice in half. Smash the rest of the garlic cloves leaving the skin on and set aside.

Using a sharp pointy knife, make incisions all over the lamb and insert the garlic halves into each one. Rub the olive oil, lemon juice, paprika, oregano, thyme, salt and pepper all over the lamb. Place the lamb onto a baking dish, scatter the smashed garlic cloves around the lamb with the skins of the juiced lemons, skin side up.

Pour water into the pan then put it in the oven and roast on high heat for 30 minutes. Reduce the temperature to 150°C (300°F), add the potatoes to the pan around the lamb and cover tightly with foil then leave to slow cook for 5½–6½ hours. Baste the lamb every now and then with the juices, if possible. Check after 5½ hours to see if lamb is cooked and very tender.

When cooked, remove from the oven and allow to rest for about 20–30 minutes before serving. Skim off any fat before serving with the lamb juices.

Spicy Moroccan Lamb

SERVES 4

SUITABLE FOR GRAZING BOARD

12 lamb loin chops or cutlets, trimmed
2 teaspoons ground cumin
1 teaspoon ground paprika
2–3 cloves garlic, finely grated
1 long red chilli, finely chopped
juice of 1 lemon
3 tablespoons finely chopped coriander (cilantro)
2 tablespoons finely chopped flat-leaf parsley
salt and freshly ground pepper
2 tablespoons olive oil

Place lamb chops into a deep dish.

Mix together all the remaining ingredients until well combined. Pour marinade over the lamb and coat completely. Place in the refrigerator and leave to marinate for about 2 hours, or longer.

Cook the chops on a preheated hot griddle pan or barbecue for 2–3 minutes each side until browned but still pink on the inside.

Serve with a sprinkle of finely chopped coriander and a squeeze of lemon juice.

Also great served with hummus (page 30).

Baked Kibbeh

SERVES 6–8

SUITABLE FOR GRAZING BOARD

250 g (9 oz) fine grit bourghul (cracked wheat)
150 g (5 oz) lean minced lamb
1 medium onion, grated
3 tablespoons chopped fresh mint
½ teaspoon chilli flakes
salt and freshly ground pepper
1 teaspoon pine nuts, to garnish
30 g (1 oz) ghee butter, melted

Filling

¼ cup pine nuts
30 g (1 oz) ghee butter
1 medium onion, finely chopped
350 g (12 oz) lean minced lamb
¼ cup sultanas
salt and freshly ground pepper
extra pine nuts, to garnish

Note: Kibbeh is made in many different ways but probably the better known are the kibbeh balls, which are balls of the bourghul mixture stuffed with the filling mixture then deep fried. This version is less time consuming to make and is baked instead of fried. Ghee butter is traditionally used as it gives a distinct flavour. Ghee is available in most large supermarkets, delicatessens and Indian/Middle Eastern specialty stores.

Cover bourghul in hot water and soak for 10 minutes, drain in a fine sieve and press with the back of a spoon to remove as much moisture as you possibly can. Place in a bowl with the lamb, onion, mint, chilli, salt and pepper and mix to combine.

To prepare the filling, dry roast the pine nuts over low–medium heat in a non-stick pan until golden and set aside. Melt the ghee in a frying pan and sauté the onion until golden, add the mince and cook on high heat until browned, breaking up any lumps. Add the pine nuts and sultanas, season with salt and pepper, cover and cook on low heat for about 5–7 minutes.

Preheat oven to 190°C (375°F) and line the base of a square 21 x 21 x 5 cm (9 x 9 x 2 in) tin with a sheet of non-stick baking paper.

Press half the bourghul mixture into the base of the tin. Spread the filling mixture evenly on top and then the remaining bourghul mixture, smoothing it out with wet hands. Score a diamond pattern on top without cutting right through and garnish by pressing a pine nut into the centre of each diamond. Pour melted ghee over the top, covering it completely, and bake for about 35–45 minutes until golden browned on top. Cut through the scored sections and serve warm.

Chorizo Sausage, Pepper and Olive Frittata

SERVES 6

SUITABLE FOR GRAZING BOARD

1 tablespoon olive oil
2 chorizo sausages, sliced
1 red onion, halved and sliced
1 red capsicum (pepper), cut into strips
1 green capsicum (pepper), cut into strips
3 shallots (scallions/spring onions), chopped
12 pitted kalamata olives
8 extra-large eggs
½ teaspoon smoked paprika
salt and freshly ground pepper

Heat oil in a medium-sized non-stick frying pan over medium heat, add the chorizo and cook for 2–3 minutes until it starts to change colour. Add the onion and cook until soft then stir in the capsicum and cook for another 3–4 minutes until the vegetables are tender. Stir in the shallots and cook for about a minute then add the olives.

Whisk the eggs with the paprika, salt and a good grind of pepper. Pour the eggs into the pan and give it a good swirl, reduce the heat to low and cook until the eggs have set at the bottom but are still runny on the top.

Meanwhile, heat your grill to medium. Place the pan under the grill for a couple of minutes until the top of the frittata is set and lightly browned. Leave to rest for 2–3 minutes and then slide the frittata onto a serving plate. Cut into wedges or pieces and serve either warm or cold.

Baked Meatballs

MAKES ABOUT 15

SUITABLE FOR GRAZING BOARD

500 g (18 oz) lean beef mince
1 medium onion, coarsely grated
2–3 cloves garlic, finely grated
3 eggs
3–4 tablespoons finely chopped flat-leaf parsley
3 tablespoons milk
1 tablespoons dried oregano
1 tablespoon extra-virgin olive oil
80 g (2½ oz) panko breadcrumbs
salt and pepper

Preheat oven to 200°C (400°F) and line two baking trays with non-stick paper.

Place the mince into a large bowl with all the remaining ingredients and mix well to combine. Shape into round balls the size of a large walnut and place on the prepared trays. Bake for 35–40 minutes.

Note: These meat balls are really delicious cold or warm. They can be used to make into a meatball sauce for spaghetti, are great in sandwiches and ideal for the grazing board. If using for a grazing board shape the meatballs smaller.

Baked Cabbage Rolls

SERVES 4–6

1 small–medium savoy cabbage

Stuffing

250 g (9 oz) beef mince
250 g (9 oz) pork mince
1 onion, finely chopped
2 cloves garlic, finely chopped
1 tablespoon tomato paste
400 g (14 oz) can peeled tomatoes, finely chopped
75 g (2½ oz) medium grain rice, rinsed
salt and freshly ground black pepper
3 tablespoons freshly chopped parsley
3 tablespoons grated parmesan cheese
2 eggs, lightly beaten

Tomato sauce

1 tablespoon extra-virgin olive oil
1 onion, finely chopped
2 cloves garlic, finely chopped
3 tablespoons tomato paste
400 g (14 oz) can diced tomatoes
250 ml (8 fl oz) water
salt and freshly ground black pepper
chopped parsley for garnish

Remove and discard the thick base from the leaves of the cabbage and blanch the whole cabbage in salted boiling water for 5 minutes then drain and separate the leaves.

Prepare the stuffing by heating the oil in a large frying pan over medium–high heat and browning the minces. Add the onion and the garlic and continue cooking until the onion is soft. Stir in the tomato paste and cook for a minute then add the tomatoes, rice, salt and pepper and cook for 10–15 minutes. Remove from the heat and cool. When cool, stir in the parsley, cheese and eggs and mix well.

Place an equal amount of the stuffing mixture at the end of each cabbage leaf and roll into a fairly large roll. Make sure that the filling is completely enclosed by tucking in the sides as you roll.

Preheat oven to 180°C (350°F).

To prepare the sauce, heat the oil in a frying pan and sauté the onion until golden. Stir in the garlic and cook for a few seconds until fragrant then stir in the tomato paste and cook for another minute. Add the tomatoes, water, salt and pepper and simmer for about 10 minutes.

Place cabbage rolls side by side in a single layer in a large baking dish and pour the tomato sauce over the rolls. Bake for about 45 minutes and serve garnished with chopped parsley.

Note: Depending on the size of the cabbage you may not have enough filling to use for the amount of cabbage that you have. Use any leftover cabbage as a salad by roughly chopping and tossing through your favourite salad dressing.

SEAFOOD

Salt Cod Fritters

SERVES 6–8

SUITABLE FOR GRAZING BOARD

750 g (27 oz) salt cod
2 large eggs
2 cloves garlic, finely grated
good handful of finely chopped flat-leaf parsley
125 g (4 oz) flour
freshly ground black pepper
olive oil for frying
lemon wedges for serving

Rinse the cod under cold running water to remove all the salt that is caked on. Place in a bowl, cover with water and leave in the fridge for 48 hours to soak, changing the water 4–5 times each day.

Drain and remove the skin and any bones. Flake or chop the flesh and place in a bowl.

Mix in the eggs, garlic, parsley, flour and lots of pepper.

Heat enough oil on medium–high heat to deep fry. Drop a tablespoonful of the cod mixture into the hot oil and fry until golden all over. Remove from the pan with a slotted spoon and drain on kitchen paper.

Serve hot with lemon wedges.

Note: These are really lovely and perfect to include on a grazing board. Don't be put off by having to soak the fish for 48 hours. This process removes most of the salt and rehydrates the cod, which makes flaking easy. You just need to organise the soaking two days before you intend to use the fritters. They are really worth it.

Prawns with Feta

SERVES 4–6

20 large green prawns
3 tablespoons olive oil
8 shallots (scallions/spring onions), chopped
3 cloves garlic, finely chopped
1 tablespoon tomato paste
400 g (14 oz) can diced tomatoes
good handful of finely chopped fresh parsley
2 teaspoons dried oregano leaves
freshly ground black pepper
125 ml (4 fl oz) dry white wine
150 g (5 oz) feta cheese, cubed
extra chopped parsley, to garnish

Peel and de-vein the prawns leaving the tail intact. Rinse, pat dry and set aside.

Heat the oil in a large pan over medium heat and fry the shallots until they just start to change colour. Stir in the garlic, cook for a few seconds then add the tomato paste and cook for another 1–2 minutes. Add the tomatoes, parsley, oregano, pepper and wine and simmer gently for approximately 15–20 minutes, until the sauce thickens. Add the prawns to the tomato sauce, cook for 5 minutes then stir in the feta and cook for another 3–5 minutes, until the feta starts to melt.

Garnish with extra chopped parsley and serve with crusty bread.

Whole Snapper with Herbed Rice and Mushrooms

SERVES 4

5 tablespoons extra-virgin olive oil
1 small onion, finely chopped
4 shallots (scallions/spring onions), chopped
1 stick celery, finely sliced
125 g (4 oz) mushrooms, sliced
2 teaspoons dried oregano leaves
2 tablespoons chopped fresh parsley
1 teaspoon paprika
180 g (6 oz) cooked long grain rice (about 1 cup)
salt and freshly ground pepper
1 whole snapper, about 1.5 kg (3 lb 5 oz), scaled and cleaned
2 tablespoons white balsamic vinegar

Garnish

1 tomato, sliced
1 onion, sliced in rings
2 shallots (scallions/spring onions), chopped
1 tablespoon chopped parsley
1 teaspoon paprika

Preheat oven to 200°C (400°F) and line a baking tray with non-stick baking paper.

Heat 3 tablespoons of the oil in a frying pan over medium heat and sauté the onion and shallots until soft. Add the celery and mushrooms and continue cooking for another 3 minutes. Stir in the oregano, parsley and paprika and cook for another minute. Remove from the heat and mix in the rice. Season with salt and pepper.

Place the fish on the prepared tray and fill with the rice mixture. Mix the balsamic vinegar and remaining 2 tablespoons of oil together and drizzle over the fish. Place in the oven and bake for 20–30 minutes.

Remove the fish from the oven and arrange alternate slices of tomato and onion over the fish. Sprinkle with the extra shallots, parsley and paprika and season with salt and pepper. Loosely cover with foil, return to the oven and continue baking for another 30 minutes or until the fish is cooked.

Octopus in Red Wine

SERVES 4

1¼ kg (2 lb 12 oz) baby octopus, cleaned
2 tablespoons olive oil
1 large brown onion, halved then finely sliced
4 cloves garlic, chopped
2 tablespoons tomato paste
1 x 400 g (14 oz) can diced tomatoes
2 tablespoons red wine vinegar
1 cup red wine
⅓ cup chopped flat-leaf parsley
salt and freshly ground black pepper

Wash the octopus thoroughly then place in a colander to drain off any excess water.

Heat the oil in a large saucepan on high heat and sauté the onion until golden. Add the garlic and cook for another minute. Stir in the octopus and cook for about 5 minutes giving it a stir every now and then. (At this stage there will be quite a bit of liquid that will come out of the octopus).

Add the tomato paste and cook for 1–2 minutes then add the tomatoes, vinegar, wine, parsley, salt and pepper. As soon as sauce starts to bubble reduce heat to medium, cover and simmer for 20 minutes. Remove lid, reduce heat and continue cooking for another 10 minutes or so until sauce is thick and octopus tender.

Serve warm or cold with lots of bread to mop up the sauce.

Note: The sauce in this recipe is delicious and thick. I usually serve this dish as a main meal either with rice or pasta.

Prawns with Charmoula

SERVES 6

SUITABLE FOR GRAZING BOARD

24 large green prawns
½ cup finely chopped coriander (cilantro)
½ cup finely chopped flat-leaf parsley
3 cloves garlic, grated
125 ml (4 fl oz) extra-virgin olive oil
grated rind of 1 lemon
125 ml (4 fl oz) lemon juice
pinch of saffron
½–1 teaspoon chilli flakes
1 teaspoon ground sweet paprika
1 teaspoon ground cumin
salt to taste

Peel and de-vein the prawns leaving the tails intact and set aside.

Combine all the remaining ingredients. Pour over the prawns, cover and refrigerate for 1–2 hours.

Heat a large non-stick frying pan over medium–high heat until hot and cook the prawns for about 2–3 minutes each side. Pour any remaining marinade into the pan for the last minute of cooking and toss through. Alternatively, the prawns can be grilled or barbecued.

Squeeze with a little lemon juice and serve with lemon wedges.

Garlic Prawns

SERVES 4–6

SUITABLE FOR GRAZING BOARD

1 kg (2.2 lb) large raw prawns
125 ml (4 fl oz) extra-virgin olive oil
30 g (1 oz) butter
4–6 cloves garlic, finely chopped
½ teaspoon chilli flakes
salt and freshly ground black pepper
juice of ½ a lemon
3 tablespoons finely chopped flat-leaf parsley

Peel and de-vein prawns leaving tails intact. Make a thin cut down the back of each prawn.

Heat the oil and butter over medium heat in a medium-sized frying pan.

Reduce heat to low and add the garlic, chilli, salt and pepper and gently cook for about 2–3 minutes until bubbly but without burning the garlic. Add the prawns, lemon juice and half the parsley. Raise heat to medium, cover and cook for about 5–7 minutes until the prawns are cooked.

Sprinkle with the remaining parsley and some more lemon juice and serve with lots of crusty bread to mop up the juices with.

Whitebait

SERVES 4

SUITABLE FOR GRAZING BOARD

500 g (18 oz) fresh whitebait fish
250 g (9 oz) flour
salt and freshly ground black pepper
light olive oil for frying
lemon wedges, to serve

Rinse the fish and pat dry with paper towel.

Heat enough oil in a deep frying pan over medium–high heat to cover the fish.

Season the flour with salt and pepper. Toss the fish in the flour, shake off any excess and fry in the hot oil until golden and crisp all over. You may need to fry the fish in batches depending on the size of your pan.

Remove from pan with a slotted spoon and drain on paper towel. Squeeze some lemon juice on top and sprinkle with salt.

Serve immediately with lemon wedges.

Note: These are eaten whole. If you can't find whitebait use whatever other tiny little fish you can find. They are really delicious and don't take too long to cook at all but must be cooked until crispy.

Spanish Prawns

SERVES 4–6

2 tablespoons extra-virgin olive oil
4 cloves garlic, sliced
1–2 long red chillies, sliced
6 shallots (scallions/spring onions), sliced
1 tablespoon fresh thyme leaves
1 teaspoon smoked paprika
½ teaspoon cinnamon
good pinch saffron strands
1 kg (35 oz) large green prawns, peeled, de-veined, tail intact
150 ml (5 fl oz) white wine
salt and pepper
2 tablespoons finely chopped flat-leaf parsley
1–2 teaspoons butter
lemon juice

Heat oil in a large frying pan over medium heat and add the garlic, chillies and shallots. Cook for 2–3 minutes, stirring regularly. Stir in the thyme, paprika, cinnamon and saffron then add the prawns and wine and season with salt and pepper. Toss well. Cook until the prawns change colour to pink and are cooked through. Make sure you stir the prawns regularly. Add a little water if the pan juices dry out. Stir in the parsley, butter and a good squeeze of lemon juice and cook for another minute or so before serving.

Whole Calamari with Savoury Rice

SERVES 4

350 g (12 oz) basmati rice
2–3 tablespoons extra-virgin olive oil
6–10 anchovies, chopped
5 cloves garlic, finely sliced
2–3 long red chillies, sliced
3 tablespoons capers, drained
good handful of roughly chopped flat-leaf parsley
90 g (3 oz) baby rocket (arugula)
12 whole baby calamari tubes
250 g (9 oz) flour
salt and freshly ground pepper
extra olive oil for frying
lemon juice, to serve
lemon wedges, to garnish

Note: If using calamari that you have cleaned yourself, cook the heads and tentacles as well.

Cook rice as you would usually and leave until needed.

Heat the oil in a large frying pan over medium heat and sauté the anchovies for 1–2 minutes until they start to break up – they will start to spit and sizzle quite a bit at this stage so take care. Stir in the garlic and chilli and cook for about 2 minutes, until the garlic starts to change colour, then add the capers and give the pan a good stir or toss. Stir in the rice and mix so as to completely coat with all the other ingredients and continue cooking long enough to heat through. Remove from the heat, toss through the parsley and rocket and keep warm while you cook the calamari.

Place a long, wide-bladed knife into each calamari tube then using a very sharp knife cut slices through the width of each one until you have a calamari that looks like a concertina. Placing the knife inside the tube enables you to cut right through just one side of the calamari without affecting the other side.

Season the flour with salt and pepper and heat enough oil in a frying pan to shallow fry. Dust the calamari in the seasoned flour and fry until golden, about 3 minutes on each side.

Serve the savoury rice on a large platter and drape the calamari on top. Squeeze some lemon juice on top and drizzle with extra-virgin olive oil. Garnish with lemon wedges.

Pickled Octopus

SERVES 6–8

SUITABLE FOR GRAZING BOARD

1 kg (2.2 lb) large octopus, cleaned
2 small and thin carrots, peeled and sliced diagonally
1–2 stalks celery, sliced
3 cloves garlic, sliced
1 red chilli, seeded and sliced (optional)
½–1 teaspoon chilli flakes
1 tablespoon dried oregano leaves
1–2 tablespoons lemon juice, to taste
60 ml (2 fl oz) red wine vinegar
180 ml (6 fl oz) extra-virgin olive oil
salt and pepper
celery leaves
parsley leaves

Place the octopus in a large saucepan, cover with cold water and bring to the boil. Reduce the heat and simmer on low for 1–1¼ hours. Turn off heat and leave to cool completely in the pot. The octopus should be very tender when cooled. Drain and reserve about half a cup of the cooking liquid.

Blanch the carrots in boiling water for 2–3 minutes then plunge in ice-cold water to stop the cooking process. Do the same with the celery but only blanch for 1 minute.

Remove any bits of loose skin from the octopus and cut into pieces. Place in a bowl with the reserved cooking liquid, carrots, celery, garlic, chilli, chilli flakes, oregano, lemon juice, vinegar and oil and season with salt and pepper. Add some of the tender celery leaves and parsley leaves and toss together to thoroughly combine.

Leave to marinate in the fridge overnight before use. Keep in a covered glass container in the fridge and use as required. Bring to room temperature before serving.

This dish is great as part of a mezze plate with other mezze dishes such as hummus, tzatziki, baba ganoush and whitebait.

Crumbed Fresh Sardines

SERVES 4–6

SUITABLE FOR GRAZING BOARD

12 large sardines
225 g (8 oz) fresh breadcrumbs
½ cup flat-leaf parsley leaves
2 eggs, lightly beaten
salt and freshly ground black pepper
75 g (2½ oz) plain flour
olive oil for frying

Clean the sardines by removing and discarding the heads. Cut along the belly, remove the insides then flatten to butterfly, cut out the backbone leaving the tail intact. You can buy these ready cleaned at most good fish shops.

To make the breadcrumbs, remove the crusts from day-old bread and place in a food processor with the parsley and process until you have green tinged breadcrumbs.

Season the egg with salt and pepper.

Dust the sardines with flour, dip in the egg then coat with the breadcrumbs, pressing lightly so that you have a generous coating of breadcrumbs on the sardines.

Heat the oil in a large frying pan and cook the sardines on medium heat for about 2 minutes each side until golden. Place on kitchen paper to drain and serve immediately with a squeeze of lemon juice.

Fried Calamari

SERVES 4–6

SUITABLE FOR GRAZING BOARD

250 g (9 oz) flour
2 teaspoons ground dried oregano
grated rind of 1 lemon
salt and freshly ground pepper
1 kg (2 lb 2 oz) calamari
light olive oil for frying
lemon wedges to serve

Mix together the flour, oregano, lemon rind, salt and pepper in a plastic bag.

Clean the calamari by gently pulling and separating the head from the hood. Pull out the insides from the calamari and remove the fine cartilage then gently pull away the very fine skin and the wings. Cut out the eyes and remove the beak, which is in the centre of the tentacles, by pushing it up and away. Cut off a small piece at the base of the hood to allow water to run through freely and clean out anything that may be left behind. Rinse thoroughly in cold water. Slice the bodies into rings about 1½ cm (⅝ in) wide. To clean the heads, cut out the eyes and the thick membrane that is near them. Keep the tentacles whole unless they are big.

Pour oil into a large frying pan to a depth of about 1½ cm (⅝ in) and heat over medium–high heat. Toss the calamari in the flour, shake off any excess and fry in batches in the hot oil until crisp and golden. Take care while frying as calamari can splatter while cooking.

Remove from the pan with a slotted spoon and drain on paper towel. Sprinkle with lemon juice and serve with lemon wedges.

Grilled Baby Octopus

SERVES 4

SUITABLE FOR GRAZING BOARD

- 1.25 kg (2 lb 12 oz) baby octopus, cleaned
- 2 tablespoons extra-virgin olive oil
- 2 tablespoons balsamic vinegar
- 2 tablespoons lemon juice
- 1 teaspoon sweet paprika
- 3 tablespoons chopped flat-leaf parsley
- 2 tablespoons dried oregano leaves
- ½–1 teaspoon chilli flakes
- freshly ground black pepper
- 1 tablespoon extra-virgin olive oil (extra)
- chopped flat-leaf parsley (extra)

Rinse the octopus, place in a colander and drain well.

Transfer the octopus to a bowl and add the olive oil, vinegar, lemon juice, paprika, parsley, oregano, chilli and pepper. Mix well and leave to marinate for 1–2 hours before cooking, preferably longer, if possible.

Heat 1 tablespoon of extra-virgin olive oil in a large frying pan. Using a slotted spoon, remove the octopus from the marinade and reserve the liquid. When the oil is hot add the octopus and cook on high heat, stirring frequently until most of the liquid evaporates. This will take about 20 minutes and the octopus will be just about cooked.

When the pan starts to dry out add the reserved marinade liquid and cook for another 5 minutes or so until the octopus is cooked and the juices are thick. Place lemon halves skin side up in the pan with the octopus. Taste and season with salt if needed.

Serve with a drizzle of extra-virgin olive oil and a little chopped parsley and or caramelised lemons.

Note: A lot of liquid will usually come out of the octopus while cooking. You need to keep cooking until all this liquid evaporates and you are left with some beautiful thick pan juices and the octopus is tender. Octopus tends to shrink a lot during cooking so you will be left with less than what you started with.

Moroccan Baked Fish with Preserved Lemons

SERVES 2

2 cloves garlic, grated
1 small piece fresh ginger, grated
½ teaspoon coriander seeds
½ teaspoon ground cumin
½ teaspoon hot or sweet paprika
3 tablespoons roughly chopped coriander
3 tablespoons roughly chopped flat-leaf parsley
2 thick fish fillets, such as ling or cod, roughly 200 g (7 oz) each
salt and freshly ground black pepper
¼ preserved lemon, thinly sliced
1 tablespoon extra-virgin olive oil
½–1 teaspoon lemon zest
good pinch saffron threads
¼ teaspoon ground cinnamon
1 tablespoon orange juice

Preheat oven to 200°C (400°F).

Combine the garlic, ginger, coriander seeds, cumin, paprika, coriander leaves and parsley in a mortar and pestle and grind until you have a thick smooth paste. Set aside. Alternatively, you can process the ingredients in a small food processor.

Sprinkle the fish with a little salt and pepper then place a few slices of the preserved lemon on the fish. Bake in the oven for about 10–12 minutes depending on the thickness of the fish, until the fish is cooked through.

In the meantime, heat the oil in a frying pan over medium heat, add the paste and cook stirring regularly for about a minute. The mixture will be very fragrant. Stir in the lemon zest, saffron, cinnamon and orange juice to make a thickish sauce. If too thick stir in a little more orange juice.

Place the fish on a serving platter, spoon over the sauce mixture, garnish with the remaining preserved lemon slices and more chopped parsley and fresh coriander leaves and serve.

Mussels in White Wine and Herbs

SERVES 4–6

1½ kg (3 lb 5 oz) raw mussels
2 teaspoons butter
2 eschalots (French shallots), finely chopped
2 shallots (scallions/spring onions), finely sliced
2–3 cloves garlic, finely sliced
180 ml (6 fl oz) dry white wine
2 sprigs of thyme
1 bay leaf
freshly ground black pepper
2–3 tablespoons chopped flat-leaf parsley

Clean and prepare the mussels by scrubbing and rinsing to remove any dirt and barnacles and by pulling off the beard. Usually, before cooking any opened mussels should be discarded as this means they are not fresh.

Melt the butter in a large saucepan, add the eschalots, shallots and garlic and cook until soft Pour in the wine, add the thyme, bay leaf and pepper, bring to the boil and boil for about 1–2 minutes. Add the mussels, cover, give the pan a good shake and cook until the mussels open. As soon as all the mussels open remove them with a slotted spoon and keep warm in a large bowl. Discard any unopened ones.

Boil the cooking liquor over high heat until reduced for about 1 minute then return the mussels to the pan add the parsley and shake the pan once or twice. Heat through and serve with lots of crusty bread.

Seafood Marinara Sauce

SERVES 4

- 3–4 tablespoons extra-virgin olive oil
- 1 medium onion, finely chopped
- 6 large cloves garlic, finely chopped
- 2 tablespoons tomato paste
- 250 ml (8 fl oz) white/rose wine
- 600 ml (20 fl oz) bottle tomato passata sauce
- 60 ml (2 fl oz) water
- salt and freshly ground black pepper
- 1.2 kg (2 lb 6 oz) seafood marinara mix
- good handful finely chopped flat-leaf parsley

Heat the oil in a large saucepan over medium heat and sauté the onion until soft and golden. Stir in the garlic and cook for about 30 seconds until fragrant. Stir in the tomato paste and cook for about 2 minutes. Pour in the wine and cook for 3–5 minutes until the alcohol evaporates then add the passata and cook for a few minutes until the sauce bubbles.

Add the water, season with salt and pepper to taste, bring to the boil then reduce the heat and cover the pan leaving the lid ajar. Simmer for 30 minutes until the sauce reduces and thickens. Add the marinara mix, bring back to the boil then reduce the heat to low and simmer for 15 minutes or until the seafood is cooked. Add the parsley, take off the heat and allow to stand for a few minutes before serving either over spaghetti or with a crusty baguette/bread and a good bottle of wine.

Note: You can use whatever combination of seafood you like if you do not want to use the ready mixed type. These days good fishmongers have great ready pre-prepared marinara mix, which is what I tend to use. Don't be afraid to use a fair bit of garlic – a marinara sauce is best with lots of garlic. Any leftover sauce is even better the day after.

For as long as I can remember my family has always served this dish with lots of grated parmesan cheese, it is really delicious. Some say cheese should not mix with seafood ... you decide!

Mustard and Dill Crusted Salmon

SERVES 4

4 salmon fillets,
approx. 200 g (7 oz) each
150 g (5 oz) fresh breadcrumbs
3 tablespoons dijon mustard
3 tablespoons chopped dill
1–2 shallots (scallions/spring onions), finely sliced including the greens
2 tablespoons chopped flat-leaf parsley
2 large cloves garlic, grated
zest of 1 lemon
2–3 tablespoons lemon juice
1–2 tablespoons olive oil
salt and freshly ground pepper

Preheat oven to 190°C (375°F). Line a baking tray with baking paper.

Trim the salmon fillets to an even shape and place skin-side down on the baking tray.

Place the breadcrumbs in a bowl with the mustard, dill, shallots, parsley, garlic, lemon zest and juice, salt and pepper and enough olive oil to form a mixture that holds together. Mix thoroughly to combine, using your hands to mix and squeeze the mixture together so it holds.

Divide the mixture in four and spread evenly on top of each fillet. Drizzle with a little extra olive oil and bake for 15–20 minutes or until the topping is golden and the salmon is cooked.

Serve with a good squeeze of lemon juice and sprigs of dill.

Oysters with Chilli, Garlic Herb Butter and Parmesan Cheese

SERVES 6–8

SUITABLE FOR GRAZING BOARD

90 g (3 oz) butter
3 shallots (scallions/spring onions) finely chopped
½–1 teaspoon chilli flakes
2–3 cloves garlic, finely grated
1 tablespoon finely chopped flat-leaf parsley
1 tablespoon finely chopped fresh chives
2 dozen large fresh oysters
grated parmesan cheese
rock salt
lemon or lime juice

Preheat oven to 190°C (375°F).

Heat the butter in a small saucepan until it melts and starts to bubble, add the shallots and cook until soft. Stir in the chilli flakes and garlic and cook for 30 seconds. Stir in the parsley and chives and cook for another minute. Remove from the heat.

Fill the bottom of a large baking tray or dish with rock salt and sit the oysters on top. The salt helps to balance the oysters. Liberally top each oyster with the herb butter then sprinkle with parmesan cheese. Bake for 5–7 minutes until heated through.

Serve with a sprinkle of lemon or lime juice.

Pan-Grilled Calamari

SERVES 4–6

SUITABLE FOR GRAZING BOARD

1 kg (2 lb 4 oz) baby calamari
2 tablespoons extra-virgin olive oil
4 cloves garlic, halved
2 tablespoons red wine vinegar
salt and freshly ground black pepper
chopped flat-leaf parsley

Clean the calamari by gently pulling and separating the head from the hood. The insides should come away with the head. Remove the fine cartilage and gently pull away the very fine skin. The wings will come away with the skin. Cut out the eyes and remove the beak, which is in the centre of the tentacles, by pushing it up and away. Cut off a small piece at the base of the hood to allow water to freely run through and clean out anything that may be left behind. Rinse the cleaned calamari thoroughly in cold water.

Heat the oil in a large frying pan until very hot, add the calamari and cook quickly on high heat until browned, turning regularly. Add the garlic cook 1–2 minutes until it takes on some colour, tossing the calamari occasionally as it cooks. Pour in the red wine vinegar. Give the pan a good swirl, season with a little salt and a good grind of pepper. Stir in the parsley and serve.

Seafood Skewers

MAKES 10 SKEWERS

SUITABLE FOR GRAZING BOARD

20 large green prawns
2 x 300 g (11 oz) salmon fillet, skin on
10 large scallops
60 ml (2 fl oz) extra-virgin olive oil
2 cloves garlic, finely grated
1 teaspoon dried oregano leaves
1 teaspoon fresh thyme leaves
½ teaspoon chilli flakes or to taste
good pinch of saffron
juice and rind of 1 lemon
salt and freshly ground black pepper
chopped fresh flat-leaf parsley, to garnish
lemon juice, to serve
10 skewers

Peel and de-vein the prawns leaving the tail intact. Cut each salmon fillet into 20 pieces leaving the skin on so that it does not fall apart during cooking.

Place the prawns, salmon, scallops, oil, garlic, oregano, thyme, chilli, saffron, lemon juice and rind in a bowl. Season with salt and pepper and toss well to combine. Refrigerate for 1–2 hours before cooking.

Thread the seafood onto small skewers allowing two prawns, two pieces of salmon and one scallop per skewer when threading as in the photo.

Cook on a hot griddle pan or under a grill for about 5–8 minutes, turning frequently until the seafood is cooked.

Serve with lemon wedges and a sprinkle of chopped parsley.

Note: If using wooden skewers, soak in cold water for at least half an hour before using to stop the skewers from burning during cooking.

POULTRY

Chicken cacciatore

SERVES 4

4 chicken thigh cutlets, bone in
salt and pepper
3 tablespoons extra-virgin olive oil
250 g (9 oz) mushrooms, sliced
1 large onion, chopped
1 red capsicum (pepper), de-seeded and sliced
1 yellow capsicum (pepper), de-seeded and sliced
4–6 cloves garlic, finely chopped
2 heaped tablespoons tomato paste
400 g (14 oz) can diced tomatoes
3 tablespoons fresh thyme leaves
1 tablespoon dried oregano
2 tablespoons chopped basil
3 tablespoons chopped flat-leaf parsley
125 ml (4 fl oz) red wine
500 ml (16 fl oz) chicken stock
125 g (4 oz) pitted kalamata olives
extra parsley, to garnish

Season the chicken well all over with salt and pepper. Heat the oil in a large heavy pan over medium–high heat and sauté the chicken on both sides until it is a deep golden colour. Remove from the pan and set aside.

Add a little more oil to the pan if necessary and cook the mushrooms until golden. Remove from the pan and add to the chicken.

Add the onion to the pan and sauté for 3–4 minutes until golden then stir in the capsicum and cook for 4–5 minutes until tender. Stir in the garlic and cook for a few seconds until fragrant. Stir in the tomato paste, cook for about a minute the add the tomatoes, herbs, wine and stock. Season with salt and a generous amount of pepper, give the pan a good stir then return the chicken and mushrooms to the pan, nestling the chicken into the sauce. Bring to the boil then reduce the heat and simmer covered for about 40–45 minutes. Add the olives, return to the heat and simmer uncovered for a further 15 minutes until the sauce has reduced and thickened.

Garnish with extra chopped parsley and serve.

Stuffed Chicken Breasts in a Red Wine Mushroom Sauce

SERVES 4

4 chicken breast fillets approx. 200–250 g (7–9 oz) each, skin removed

Sauce
3 tablespoons olive oil
1 medium onion, chopped
2 cloves garlic, chopped
2 heaped tablespoons tomato paste
1 teaspoon sugar
1 x 400 g (14 oz) can diced tomatoes
1 tablespoon chopped fresh parsley
250 ml (8 fl oz) water
125 ml (4 fl oz) red wine
salt and pepper
250 g (9 oz) button mushrooms, thinly sliced

Filling
45 g (1½ oz) sun-dried tomatoes, chopped
8–10 black olives, seeded and chopped
1 tablespoon chopped fresh parsley
2 tablespoons chopped fresh chives
125 g (4 oz) fresh breadcrumbs
salt and freshly ground pepper
1 teaspoon dried oregano leaves
1 egg

To prepare the sauce, heat the oil in a saucepan and sauté the onion and garlic until golden. Stir in the tomato paste and sugar and cook for 1 minute. Add the tomatoes, parsley, water, wine, salt and pepper and cook for another 2–3 minutes. Stir in the mushrooms, cover, reduce the heat and simmer for 20 minutes. Remove from the heat and allow to cool.

Preheat the oven to 200°C (400°F).

Prepare the filling by combing all the ingredients until you have a mixture that holds together.

Using a sharp knife, cut a deep incision along the length of the chicken fillet to make a deep pocket. Divide the stuffing mixture into four portions and fill each chicken pocket tightly with the mixture. Secure each opening with a tooth pick.

Pour some of the sauce in the bottom of an ovenproof baking dish. Arrange the chicken fillets on top then pour over the remaining sauce. Bake for 30–40 minutes until the chicken is cooked and tender. If you find that sauce is drying out, add a little extra water.

Allow the chicken to rest for 10–15 minutes before serving with a drizzle of extra-virgin olive oil and green vegetables.

Chicken in Wine and Chestnuts

SERVES 2

2 chicken breast fillets, about 250 g (9 oz) each
1 teaspoon paprika
2 tbsp extra virgin olive oil
1 medium onion, finely chopped
3 cloves garlic, finely chopped
2–3 teaspoons Dijon mustard
180ml (6 fl oz) white wine
1 heaped tbsp fresh thyme leaves
380ml (12 fl oz) hot chicken stock
8–10 chestnuts, roasted and peeled
salt and pepper

Coat chicken with the paprika, heat oil in a large deep frying pan and brown chicken on both sides, remove from pan and set aside.

Add the onion and garlic to the pan; you may need to add a little more oil and sauté until golden.

Stir in the Dijon mustard then pour in the wine and allow to boil for about a minute until the alcohol evaporates.

Add the thyme leaves and stock and return chicken to the pan.

Break the chestnuts in half or quarters and scatter around the chicken, season with salt and pepper to taste

Cover, reduce heat and cook on low heat for 20–30 minutes until the chicken is cooked through and the sauce thickens.

To roast chestnuts: Chestnuts can be roasted over hot coals, on a BBQ over a gas hob or in an oven.

Cut a cross along the rounded side of the chestnut, this stops them for exploding during roasting regardless of which way they are cooked

Either place them on a rack over a fire or bake in a pre-heated 200°/400° oven on a baking sheet lined with baking paper for about 20 minutes until the skins have opened up to reveal the yellowy flesh.

Italian Chicken Parcels

SERVES 4

3 large tomatoes, thickly sliced
basil leaves
2 large cloves garlic, finely grated
salt and freshly ground black pepper
4 shallots (scallions/spring onions), sliced lengthways into thin strips
4 chicken breast fillets, skin removed and trimmed
sprigs thyme
sliced black olives
shaved parmesan cheese
extra-virgin olive oil
lemon juice

Note: This is a lovely way to cook chicken as it cooks in its own juices and so remains moist. The amount of olives and thyme used in each incision depends on your personal taste and the amount of juices in the parcel will vary depending on the tomatoes used. The parcels can be made in advance and kept in the fridge ready to be baked. Take out of the fridge 10–15 minutes before baking.

Preheat oven to 190°C (375°F).

Cut four equal-sized sheets of foil and four sheets of non-stick baking paper large enough to wrap around and hold the chicken and other ingredients. Place a sheet of non-stick baking paper on top of a sheet of foil. Do that with all the sheets so you have four sets.

Place slices of tomatoes in the middle of the baking paper and insert a basil leaf in between each slice. Sprinkle with a little bit of garlic and season to taste then scatter some shallots on top.

Make three incisions across each chicken fillet and fill each incision with sprigs of thyme, olives and parmesan cheese. Scatter extra parmesan cheese on top of the chicken and place on top of the shallots. Squeeze lemon juice over the chicken, season to taste with salt and pepper and drizzle with a little olive oil.

Bring together all the sides of the paper and foil on top of the chicken and twist to form a tight parcel. Place upright in a baking dish so the juices don't run out. Repeat the process until you have four parcels.

Bake for about 25–30 minutes then allow to stand for 5–7 minutes before serving with a drizzle of extra-virgin olive oil.

Spicy Chicken Wings

SERVES 4–6

SUITABLE FOR GRAZING BOARD

½ teaspoon saffron strands
2 teaspoons boiling water
12 large chicken wings
2 teaspoons olive oil
2 cloves garlic, finely grated
1½ teaspoons smoked paprika
1½ teaspoons ground cumin
1 teaspoon ground dried oregano
½–1 teaspoon chilli powder
1 teaspoon salt
freshly ground black pepper
lime juice

Soak the saffron strands in the boiling water for about 5 minutes.

Using a sharp knife or poultry shears separate the wings into three pieces. Discard the tip and place the other two parts of the wing in a bowl. Pour the saffron water and oil over the wings and coat well.

Mix the garlic, paprika, cumin, oregano, chilli, salt and pepper together and rub into the wings until they are completely covered. Leave to marinate in the fridge for a few hours, even overnight.

Preheat the oven to 190°C (375°F) and line a large baking tray with baking paper. Place the chicken in a single layer on the baking tray and bake for about 20 minutes each side until the wings are a deep golden colour. Serve with a squeeze of lime juice.

Chicken Kebabs with Garlic, Coriander and Lime

SERVES 6–8

SUITABLE FOR GRAZING BOARD

24 chicken tenderloins
3 cloves garlic, grated
1–2 red chillies, de-seeded and finely chopped (or 1–2 teaspoons dried chilli flakes)
½ cup finely chopped fresh coriander
2 tablespoons olive oil
1 teaspoon sweet paprika
juice and rind of 1 lime
salt and freshly ground pepper
small wooden skewers
lime wedges, to serve

Trim the chicken by removing the little sinews then place into a large bowl. Add the garlic, chilli, coriander, olive oil, paprika, lime juice and rind and season with salt and pepper to taste. Mix well so that all the chicken is completely covered with the marinade, cover and refrigerate for 1 hour before cooking.

In the meantime, soak the wooden skewers in cold water until ready to use. Thread each tenderloin onto a skewer and cook under a hot grill or on a hot griddle pan or barbecue for about 2 minutes each side until lightly browned and cooked through.

Serve with caramelised lime wedges dusted with paprika.

Moroccan Roast Chicken

SERVES 4

2 kg (4 lb 6 oz) whole chicken
5 cm (2 in) piece fresh turmeric, or 1 tablespoon ground turmeric
1 bunch coriander (cilantro)
4–5 large cloves garlic, roughly chopped
1 teaspoon salt
3 teaspoons ground cumin
1 teaspoon ground coriander
1 teaspoon ground paprika
1 teaspoon chilli flakes or 1 long red chilli, finely chopped
juice of 1 lime
2 tablespoons extra-virgin olive oil
salt, coriander and lime juice, to serve

Prepare the chicken by removing any fat from the cavity and tucking the wings in. Tie the bottom part of the drumsticks together to keep the shape during cooking. With your fingertips gently separate the skin from the breast area.

Coarsely grate the turmeric and roughly chop the coriander, including all the stalks and roots (the roots of the coriander contain the most flavour just make sure all the dirt is washed out). Place the turmeric, coriander, garlic, salt, ground cumin, ground coriander, paprika, chilli flakes, lime juice and oil in a food processor and process until you have a fine paste. Alternatively, you can prepare the paste in a mortar and pestle.

Rub the paste all over and inside the chicken, including under the skin of the breast, cover and refrigerate to marinate for least 3 hours, preferably overnight.

Take the chicken out of the fridge 30–60 minutes before cooking to bring back to room temperature. Preheat the oven to 200°C (400°F). Place the chicken in a baking dish with enough water to cover the bottom of the dish and roast for about 90 minutes until cooked, regularly basting the chicken with the juices. The chicken is cooked when the juices run clear after a skewer is inserted in the thigh area. Do not allow the pan to dry out and add more water during cooking, if necessary.

Cover the chicken with foil and allow to rest for 20 minutes before serving garnished with a sprinkling of salt, fresh coriander leaves and a squeeze of lime juice.

Caramelise wedges of lime are a great addition.

Chicken Tagine with Olives and Preserved Lemon

SERVES 4

½ teaspoon saffron threads
250 ml (8 fl oz) hot chicken stock
8 chicken thigh cutlets or 1 whole chicken cut into 8 pieces
ground paprika
1–2 tablespoons extra-virgin olive oil or ghee butter
2 large onions, peeled, halved and thinly sliced
5 cloves garlic, sliced
½ teaspoon ground ginger
¾ teaspoon ground turmeric
1 teaspoon ground cumin
1 teaspoon ground paprika
1 cinnamon stick
handful pitted kalamata olives
handful stuffed green olives
1 preserved lemon, seeded and chopped
2 tablespoons finely chopped flat-leaf parsley
juice of ½ a lemon, or to taste

Mix the saffron threads with the stock and leave to infuse.

Pat the chicken pieces dry with paper towel and lightly coat with a little ground paprika.

Heat the oil or ghee in a large deep frying pan over medium–high heat and brown the chicken on all sides then remove from the pan and set aside. Add the onions to the pan and cook until lightly browned and soft. Stir in the garlic, cook until fragrant then add the ginger, turmeric, cumin and paprika and cook for another 30 seconds.

Return the chicken to the pan, arrange on top of the onion mixture, add the cinnamon stick and scatter the olives and preserved lemon around the chicken. Scatter half the parsley on top. Pour in the stock, cover and cook on low heat for 30–40 minutes until the chicken is cooked. Stir in the lemon juice, scatter the remaining parsley on top and serve over a bed of couscous.

Baked Chicken with Oregano and Garlic

SERVES 4

1.5 kg (3 lb 5 oz) fresh whole chicken
juice of 1–1½ lemons
extra-virgin olive oil
2 teaspoons dried oregano leaves
1 teaspoon ground sweet paprika
salt and pepper
6 large cloves garlic, unpeeled
250 ml (8 fl oz) water

Note: Remove any excess oil from the roasting pan by skimming with a spoon so you are left with just a delicious chicken gravy.

Preheat oven to 200°C (400°F).

Rinse the chicken under cold running water and remove any excess fat from the cavity area and neck. Pat thoroughly dry with kitchen paper and tuck the wing tips behind the wings to prevent burning during cooking.

Place the chicken in a roasting pan, rub all over including the inside cavity with the lemon juice, a little olive oil, oregano, paprika, salt and pepper.

Smash the garlic cloves, leave them unpeeled and scatter around the chicken. Place the squeezed lemon halves in the pan cut side down and one half in the chicken cavity. Tie the bottom of the drumsticks together to keep the shape during cooking.

Cover the bottom of the pan with the water. Bake for about 1½ hours or until the chicken is completely cooked. Baste regularly with the pan juices during cooking, adding more water if the roasting pan dries out. The chicken is cooked when the juices run clear after a skewer is inserted into the thick part of the thigh.

When cooked, remove from the oven, cover with foil and allow to rest for at least half an hour.

Spanish Chicken with Rice and Chorizo

SERVES 4

½ teaspoon smoked paprika
1 teaspoon garlic powder
salt and pepper
4 chicken thigh cutlets, skinless
1–2 tablespoons extra-virgin olive oil
2 chorizo sausages, sliced
1 large brown onion, chopped
4–5 cloves garlic, finely chopped
1 large red capsicum (pepper), cut into strips
1½ cups medium grain rice
750 ml (24 fl oz) hot chicken stock
125 ml (4 fl oz) white wine
½–1 teaspoon saffron strands
zest of 1 lemon
salt and freshly ground black pepper
200 g (7 oz) stuffed green olives
good handful chopped flat-leaf parsley
lemon juice

Mix together the paprika, garlic powder, salt and pepper. Rub the chicken with the paprika mixture until well coated then set aside.

Heat the oil in a large deep frying pan over medium heat and sauté the chorizo sausage on both sides. Remove from the pan and set aside. Add the chicken to the pan and cook until it's a deep golden colour on both sides. Remove from the pan and set aside with the chorizo sausage. Keep warm by covering with foil.

Add the onion to the pan and cook until soft then stir in the garlic and capsicum and cook for 2–3 minutes. Stir in the rice, stock, wine, saffron and lemon zest and season well with salt and pepper.

Return the chicken pieces and chorizo to the pan and nestle into the rice. Bring to the boil then reduce the heat, cover and simmer for about 20–25 minutes until the rice and chicken are cooked. Scatter the olives over the chicken, cover and simmer for another 5–8 minutes until all the liquid is absorbed.

Take off the heat and leave to stand for 5–10 minutes before serving with parsley and a good sprinkle of lemon juice.

Note: This is one of those quick and really easy-to-prepare meals that are perfect for dinner after work or when unexpected guests drop by.

Herbed Roast Chicken with 40 Cloves of Garlic

SERVES 4

2 kg (4 lb 6 oz) fresh chicken
salt
3 tablespoons extra-virgin olive oil
1 teaspoon dried sage
1 teaspoon dried rosemary
1 teaspoon dried thyme
1 teaspoon dried oregano leaves
3 tablespoons flat-leaf parsley, finely chopped
2 sprigs parsley
40 large cloves garlic, whole and unpeeled
freshly ground pepper
150 ml (5 fl oz) white wine

Preheat oven to 190°C (375°F).

Remove excess fat from the chicken and rub all over with salt and olive oil, including the inside of the chicken.

Mix the sage, rosemary, thyme, oregano and chopped parsley together. Place half the herb mixture inside the chicken along with the parsley and six cloves of garlic. Tie the bottom part of the drumsticks together to keep the shape during cooking. Rub the remaining herb mixture all over the chicken and place in a baking dish that has been greased with a little olive oil. Arrange the remaining garlic around the chicken. Pour the wine over the chicken. Cover with foil or a lid and bake for 1 hour. Remove cover and bake for approximately 30 minutes more until the chicken is cooked and golden brown.

Note: Don't be put off by the amount of garlic used. This is a very popular French dish and really delicious. Once cooked in its skin the garlic loses that pungent flavour and becomes very sweet and mellow. The chicken is usually served with slices of toasted baguette that each person spreads with the garlic puree squeezed from the cloves.

Chicken with Leeks and Mustard Sauce

SERVES 4

2 tablespoons olive oil
4 chicken breast fillets, skinned
2 leeks, washed and sliced
3 cloves garlic, chopped
2 tablespoons dijon mustard
200 ml (7 fl oz) white wine
150 ml (5 fl oz) chicken stock
2 tablespoons fresh thyme leaves
200 ml (7 fl oz) cream
salt and freshly ground pepper

Heat the oil in a large, deep frying pan over medium–high heat. Add the chicken and brown on both sides then remove from the pan, cover and keep warm.

Add the leek to the pan and sauté until tender. Stir in the garlic and cook for another minute. Stir in the mustard then pour in the wine, stock, thyme and cream. Return the chicken to the pan and cook for about 1–2 minutes until the alcohol evaporates. Season with salt and pepper, stir well and bring to the boil. Reduce the heat, cover and simmer for about 15–20 minutes until the chicken is cooked and the sauce has thickened. If the sauce is too runny, cook uncovered for another 2 minutes or so until the sauce thickens.

Serve with rice or mashed potatoes.

Chicken Livers and Pancetta in Marsala Wine

SERVES 4

500 g (18 oz) chicken livers
1 tablespoon olive oil
1 tablespoon butter
1 small red onion, finely chopped
1 clove garlic, chopped
3 slices pancetta, chopped
salt and freshly ground pepper
100 ml (3½ fl oz) Marsala wine
lemon juice
chopped flat-leaf parsley

Trim and clean the chicken livers leaving them whole (if they are very large cut them in half).

Heat the oil and melt the butter in a frying pan and sauté the onion and garlic until soft. Stir in the pancetta and cook for 1–2 minutes then add the livers and sauté quickly on high heat until brown on the outside and slightly pink on the inside. Season with salt and a good grind of pepper, pour in the Marsala wine and cook for 3–4 minutes until you get a rich, thick sauce.

Serve with a squeeze of lemon juice and a sprinkle of chopped parsley.

VEGETARIAN

Quick Cheese Pie

SERVES 4

SUITABLE FOR GRAZING BOARD

200 g (7 oz) feta cheese, coarsely grated (see note below)
375 g (13 oz) cottage cheese
30 g (1 oz) grated parmesan cheese
3 eggs, beaten
1½ teaspoons dried oregano leaves
freshly ground black pepper
melted butter, for greasing
2 sheets ready rolled puff pastry
sesame seeds

Preheat oven to 200°C (400°F).

Mix together the feta, cottage and parmesan cheese. Add the eggs, oregano and pepper and mix well.

Brush the bottom of a 23 cm (9 in) round pie plate with the melted butter and line with one sheet of the pastry. Pour the mixture on top. Cover with the other sheet of pastry, brush with melted butter and sprinkle with sesame seeds. Using your fingertips, sprinkle the top of the pie with a little water – this stops the pastry from drying out.

Bake for 20–30 minutes, until the pastry is golden brown. Serve warm with a salad.

Note: This pie can be prepared well in advance and frozen for future use. There's no need to defrost first, but it will take around 45–60 minutes to cook. I always prefer to grate the feta, regardless of how soft or firm it is, as you need to get a fine texture. I would not recommend crumbling it; if your feta is very creamy and soft you might be able to mash it with a fork.

VEGETARIAN

Shakshuka

SERVES 2

2 tablespoons extra-virgin olive oil
1 medium red onion, halved and finely sliced
½ red capsicum (pepper), cored and sliced
½ green capsicum (pepper), cored and sliced
2 cloves garlic, finely chopped
1 heaped teaspoon ground cumin
1 teaspoon ground paprika
1 x 400 g (14 oz) can diced tomatoes
180 ml (6 fl oz) water
chilli to taste (optional)
salt and freshly ground pepper
10–12 pitted kalamata olives
4 large eggs
chopped flat-leaf parsley

Heat the oil in a large non-stick frying pan and sauté the onion until soft. Add the peppers and continue cooking for 3–5 minutes then stir in the garlic and cook until fragrant, about 30 seconds Stir in the cumin and paprika and cook for a minute to release the oils of the spices. Stir in the tomatoes, water, chilli if using and season with salt and pepper. Cover and simmer for about 15 minutes until the sauce has thickened.

Stir in the olives and make four indentations in the tomato mixture. Crack an egg into each one and simmer for 5–8 minutes until the eggs set to your liking.

Sprinkle with freshly chopped parsley and serve with crusty bread.

Note: Sliced chorizo sausage can be added to this dish by browning slices of chorizo in the oil before cooking the onions. Remove from the pan and set aside then return to the pan when you add the olives.

Spinach and Rice in Red Sauce

SERVES 4–6 **VEGAN**

3–4 tablespoons extra-virgin olive oil
1 large onion, finely chopped
3 cloves garlic, finely chopped
1 tablespoon tomato paste
½ teaspoon sugar
2 x 400 g (14 oz) cans diced tomatoes
375 ml (12 fl oz) water
2 bunches English spinach, washed and finely chopped
salt and freshly ground pepper
150 g (5 oz) medium grain rice
lemon juice, to serve

Heat the oil in a large saucepan and sauté the onion on medium heat until golden. Stir in the garlic and cook for about 30 seconds until fragrant. Stir in the tomato paste and sugar, cook for about 1 minute then add the undrained tomatoes and water. Reduce the heat, cover and simmer for about 10 minutes. Increase the heat and add the spinach a little at a time while stirring through the sauce so that the spinach collapses. Season with salt and pepper, cover, reduce heat to low and simmer for 20 minutes.

Stir in the rice and simmer for another 20 minutes, switch off the heat and leave to stand for 10 minutes before serving with a squeeze of lemon juice.

Note: This is very much like a risotto except that there is no stirring needed during cooking. It can be eaten straight away, warm or at room temperature.

Artichoke Hearts with Broad Beans and Lemon

SERVES 4–6

VEGAN

4 tablespoons extra-virgin olive oil
1 large brown onion, halved and thinly sliced
4 cloves garlic, sliced
1 kg (35 oz) frozen artichoke hearts, thawed
500 g (18 oz) frozen broad beans
juice of 1½–2 lemons
250 ml (8 fl oz) water
salt and freshly ground pepper
handful chopped flat-leaf parsley

Heat the oil in a large saucepan over medium heat and sauté the onion until soft. Add the garlic and cook for another minute. Add the artichoke hearts, beans, lemon juice and water. Season with salt and pepper, reduce the heat and simmer for 40–50 minutes until the artichokes and beans are tender. Stir in the parsley, adjust the seasoning and simmer for a further 2 minutes. If juices dry out during cooking add a little more water.

Serve as is or with rice.

Note: Frozen artichoke hearts are available from Middle Eastern grocery shops and some delicatessens.

Eggplant Parmigiana

SERVES 4–6

1½ kg (3 lb 5 oz) eggplant (aubergine), about 3 large
extra-virgin olive oil
salt
250 g (9 oz) mozzarella cheese, coarsely grated
150 g (5 oz) grated parmesan cheese
fresh basil leaves

Tomato sauce

60 ml (2 fl oz) extra-virgin olive oil
4 large cloves garlic, coarsely grated
800 g (28 oz) can diced tomatoes
1 teaspoon dried oregano
salt and freshly ground pepper

Preheat the oven to 200°C (400°F). Line two large baking trays with non-stick baking paper.

Top and tail the eggplants then cut into thickish slices lengthways and place onto the prepared trays. Brush each eggplant on both sides with extra-virgin olive oil and sprinkle with salt. Bake for 30–40 minutes until the eggplant is soft, browned and has collapsed.

In the meantime, make the sauce by heating the oil in a saucepan on medium heat. Add the garlic and cook until it just starts to change colour, being careful not to burn. Add the undrained tomatoes, oregano, and season with salt and pepper. Bring to the boil, reduce the heat and with the lid slightly ajar simmer on medium heat for 15 minutes.

To assemble the parmigiana, pour some of the sauce into the bottom of a 30 x 21 x 6 cm (12 x 8 x 2½ in) baking dish, then arrange a layer of eggplant, scatter some basil leaves on top and sprinkle with some of the mozzarella and parmesan. Repeat the layering process until all ingredients are used ending with the basil leaves, mozzarella and parmesan cheese.

Bake in a preheated 190°C (375°F) oven for about 20–30 minutes until golden on top and bubbly. Leave to stand for at least 30 minutes to allow the eggplant to absorb some of the sauce before serving. Always best the next day.

Zucchini Potato and Herb Tortilla

SERVES 4–6

SUITABLE FOR GRAZING BOARD

100 ml (3½ fl oz) extra-virgin olive oil
3 medium potatoes, peeled and cubed
2 onions finely sliced
2 cloves garlic, finely chopped
2 medium zucchini (courgettes), thinly sliced
½ teaspoon paprika
8 eggs
2 tablespoons chopped flat-leaf parsley
salt and freshly ground black pepper

Heat oil in a medium-size non-stick frying pan and cook the potatoes on medium heat, turning often until tender and slightly golden. Using a slotted spoon remove potatoes from the pan.

Add the onion to the pan and cook until soft. Add the garlic and zucchini and cook for about 5 minutes until the zucchini is tender. Return the potatoes to the pan and stir in the paprika.

Beat the eggs then mix in the parsley. Season with salt and pepper and pour over the vegetables. Swirl the pan and cook over a very gentle heat until the eggs start to set. Place the pan under a preheated medium–hot grill and finish cooking the tortilla until golden and completely set.

Serve the tortilla at room temperature cut into thick wedges.

Note: This tortilla is great cut into bite size pieces for a grazing board.

Fennel Baked Potatoes

SERVES 6

VEGAN

2 large fennel bulbs
2 medium onions
1 kg (35 oz) potatoes
100 ml (3½ fl oz) extra-virgin olive oil
salt and freshly ground pepper

Preheat oven to 190°C (375°F).

Remove and discard the outer leaves of the fennel and the hard core, cut in half then slice. Peel the onions, cut in half then slice. Peel the potatoes and cut into thick wedges.

Place the fennel, onions and potatoes in a large baking dish. Drizzle the vegetables with the oil and season with salt and pepper, making sure that all the vegetables are well coated. Cover with foil and bake for about 45 minutes. Remove the foil, give the vegetables a good toss and bake for a further 15–20 minutes until the potatoes are cooked.

Greek Baked Potatoes

VEGAN

1.5 kg (3 lb 5 oz) potatoes, peeled
3 cloves garlic, smashed
juice of 1 lemon
2–3 teaspoons dried oregano leaves
100 ml (3½ fl oz) extra-virgin olive oil
salt and freshly ground pepper
125 ml (4 fl oz) water

Preheat oven to 200°C (400°F).

Peel the potatoes and depending on their size cut in half or into quarters. Place in a baking dish with the garlic, lemon juice, oregano, oil, salt and pepper and mix well to completely coat the potatoes. Slowly pour in the water from the side of the baking dish so that the water does not cover the potatoes. Cover with foil and bake for 30 minutes then remove the foil and bake for another 30–35 minutes until the potatoes are cooked. Allow the potatoes to rest for 10 minutes or so.

When cooked the potatoes should be soft, if the water completely evaporates, I like to add about 2–3 tablespoons of water to the pan, swish the pan around then drizzle the juices over the potatoes when serving.

Cauliflower Patties

MAKES ABOUT 16 PATTIES

SUITABLE FOR GRAZING BOARD

- 1 small cauliflower, about 500 g (18 oz)
- 2 eggs, lightly beaten
- 2 tablespoons finely chopped flat-leaf parsley
- 2 cloves garlic, finely grated
- 1 heaped teaspoon ground cumin
- salt and freshly ground black pepper
- 75 g (2½ oz) flour
- olive oil for shallow frying

Boil the cauliflower in salted water until tender, drain and place in a bowl to cool. Chop into small pieces and use a fork to lightly mash. Mix in the egg, parsley, garlic, cumin, salt and pepper. Stir in the flour a little at a time and mix well. The mixture should not be too dry.

Heat oil in a frying pan until medium–hot, drop spoonfuls of cauliflower into the oil and cook until golden on both sides. Remove from the pan with a slotted spoon and drain on paper towel. The patties can be served hot or cold.

Bean Patties with Yoghurt and Mint Sauce

SERVES 4–6

2 x 400 g (14 oz) cans red kidney beans
3 cloves garlic, grated
4 shallots (scallions/spring onions), finely sliced
1 teaspoon ground cumin
½–1 teaspoon chilli powder
3 tablespoons chopped fresh coriander (cilantro)
1 egg
75 g (2½ oz) flour
salt to taste
2 tablespoons olive oil

Yoghurt mint sauce

200 g (7 oz) Greek yoghurt
2 tablespoons finely chopped fresh mint
1 tablespoon extra-virgin olive oil
salt and freshly ground black pepper

Drain and rinse the kidney beans, place in a bowl and coarsely mash with a fork or potato masher. Add the garlic, shallots, cumin, chilli, coriander, egg and flour and season with salt. Mix until all the ingredients are well combined.

Divide the mixture into four to six portions and shape into round patties. Heat the oil in a non-stick frying pan over medium heat. Add the patties and cook until golden on both sides, about 3–4 minutes each side.

To make the yoghurt mint sauce: Combine all the ingredients and season with salt if necessary.

Serve the patties with the yoghurt mint sauce and a garden salad.

Middle Eastern Spiced Lentils with Spinach

SERVES 2–4

VEGAN

2 tablespoons olive oil
1 onion, finely chopped
2 tablespoons tomato paste
2 x 400 g (14 oz) cans brown lentils, drained
250 g (9 oz) frozen chopped spinach
250 ml (8 fl oz) water
salt and pepper

Garnish

2–3 tablespoons extra-virgin olive oil
1 small onion, finely chopped
4 cloves garlic, grated
2 teaspoons ground cumin
½ teaspoon ground coriander

Heat the oil in a saucepan on medium–high heat and sauté the onion for 2–3 minutes. Stir in the tomato paste and cook for 2 minutes. Add the lentils, spinach, water, salt and pepper and simmer for 10–15 minutes until the spinach is cooked.

Meanwhile, prepare the garnish by heating the oil in a small frying pan and cooking the onion until it is a dark golden colour. Stir in the garlic and cook for 30 seconds. Stir in the dry spices and cook for 1 minute.

When the lentils are cooked, stir in the garnish, simmer for another 2 minutes and serve with rice.

Note: Traditionally the lentils are served with a sprinkle of brown vinegar stirred through.

Felafel

MAKES ABOUT 24 FELAFELS

VEGAN

- 200 g (7 oz) dried broad beans
- 200 g (7 oz) dried chickpeas (garbanzos)
- 2 teaspoons bicarbonate of soda
- 6 shallots (scallions/spring onions), chopped
- 4 cloves garlic, chopped
- 2 teaspoons ground cumin
- 2 teaspoons ground coriander
- ½ cup roughly chopped flat-leaf parsley
- ¾ cup fresh coriander (cilantro)
- salt and pepper
- ½–1 teaspoon chilli powder
- sesame seeds
- olive oil for deep frying

Soak the broad beans, chickpeas and 1 teaspoon of the bicarbonate of soda in plenty of cold water for 24 hours. Drain and remove the skins from the broad beans – the skins will peel off very easily. Place the broad beans, chickpeas and all the remaining ingredients except for the sesame seeds into a food processor, season to taste with salt, pepper and chilli, and process until you have a fine textured paste that holds its shape when you press it together. Cover and chill for about an hour, although this is not essential.

Shape mixture into round patties. Lightly press some sesame seeds into both sides and fry the felafels in hot oil until golden brown. Drain on paper towels.

Serve with hummus (page 30).

Persian Eggs with Lentils and Spinach

SERVES 2

- 2 tablespoons extra-virgin olive oil
- 1 medium red onion, finely chopped
- 2 cloves garlic, finely chopped
- 1 teaspoon ground cumin
- 1 teaspoon ground turmeric or 1 tablespoon freshly grated turmeric
- ½ teaspoon ground allspice
- 400 g (14 oz) can diced tomatoes
- 400 g (14 oz) can brown lentils, drained and rinsed
- chilli to taste (optional)
- 180 ml (6 fl oz) water
- 125 g (4 oz) fresh baby spinach
- salt and freshly ground pepper
- 4 large eggs
- chopped parsley

Heat oil in a large non-stick frying pan on medium heat and sauté onion until golden then add garlic and cook until fragrant, about 30 seconds. Stir in the cumin, turmeric and allspice and add the tomatoes, lentils and chilli, if using. Pour in the water and simmer, covered, for about 10–15 minutes until the sauce has thickened. Stir in the spinach, season with salt and pepper and cook until the spinach has wilted.

Make four indentations in the lentils and crack an egg into each one. Cover with a lid and simmer for a few minutes until the eggs set to your liking. Sprinkle with fresh chopped parsley and serve with crusty bread.

Black-Eyed Beans with Cumin and Potatoes

SERVES 4

VEGAN

350 g (12 oz) dried black-eyed beans
2–3 tablespoons extra-virgin olive oil
1 large brown onion, chopped
3–4 cloves garlic, chopped
1 tablespoon cumin seeds
3 teaspoons ground cumin
1½ teaspoons ground coriander
½–1 teaspoon dried chilli flakes
2 heaped tablespoons tomato paste
300 g (11 oz) small potatoes, unpeeled and halved
2 cups water
handful chopped flat-leaf parsley
lemon juice and Greek yoghurt (or Vegan substitute), to serve

Rinse the beans under cold running water (black-eyed beans don't need to be soaked), place in a saucepan, cover with water and cook for 10 minutes then drain.

Heat the oil in a saucepan and sauté the onion on medium heat until golden then add the garlic and cook until fragrant. Stir in the spices and cook for about a minute. Add the tomato paste, stir well and cook for another couple of minutes. Add the drained beans, potatoes and water, season with salt, bring to the boil. Reduce the heat, cover and simmer for about 30–40 minutes until the beans and potatoes are tender. Stir in the parsley, take off the heat and leave to rest for 10 minutes before serving.

Serve with lemon juice and/or a dollop of Greek yoghurt.

Zucchini and Haloumi Fritters

MAKES 18–20

SUITABLE FOR GRAZING BOARD

350 g (12 oz) zucchini (courgette)
150 g (5 oz) haloumi cheese, coarsely grated
1 tablespoon grated parmesan cheese
1 small red onion, finely chopped
75 g (2½ oz) plain flour
2 tablespoons chopped mint
2 eggs
freshly ground black pepper
salt to taste
olive oil for frying

Coarsely grate the zucchini, place in a colander and squeeze out as much moisture as possible. Transfer the zucchini to a large bowl. Add the haloumi, parmesan, onion, flour, mint, eggs and pepper and mix to combine. Check the seasoning and add salt if you think necessary (haloumi can be quite salty). If the mixture seems a bit too watery add a little extra flour.

Heat oil in a frying pan over medium heat. Drop spoonfuls of zucchini mixture into the pan and cook for about 2 minutes each side, until golden. Remove from the pan and drain on kitchen paper.

Serve while still warm as the haloumi can become rubbery if left too long.

VEGETARIAN

Stuffed Artichokes

SERVES 3–6

VEGAN

6 artichokes
juice of 1 lemon
3 tablespoons extra-virgin olive oil
250 g (8 oz) medium grain rice
2 large tomatoes, grated
1 onion, grated
2 cloves garlic, grated
3 tablespoons chopped dill
2 tablespoons chopped flat-leaf parsley
3 tablespoons extra-virgin olive oil
juice of ½–1 lemon
salt and freshly ground black pepper
lemon juice and dill, to serve

Prepare the artichokes by cutting off the stems close to the base and cut a very thin slice off the bottom for stability. Remove the tough outer leaves and trim around the base to neaten, trim the tops and sharp leaf ends with scissors. Carefully spread the centre leaves and gently scrape off the choke (furry centre) but do not remove the centre leaves. As you prepare each artichoke, soak in a bowl of water with the juice of one lemon to stop discolouration.

Mix all the stuffing ingredients together and fill the centres and in between the leaves with the stuffing. Place close together in a single layer in a saucepan. Add the oil, lemon juice and enough water to come halfway up the artichokes. Bring to the boil, reduce the heat and simmer, covered, for about 45 minutes until the rice is cooked and liquid has been reduced.

Serve with a sprinkle of lemon juice and fresh dill.

Note: How to eat an artichoke
If you are not sure how to handle eating an artichoke here are a few tips. The actual artichoke is eaten with your fingers. You only need to use a fork for the stuffing and the heart of the artichoke. Using your fingers, pull out each outer leaf one by one until you work your way to the heart. Place the bottom part of the leaf, which is also the thickest part of the leaf, in your mouth, and scrape off the flesh with your teeth. Discard the leaf and eat the flesh. You do this until all of the leaves are eaten and then you eat the heart of the artichoke. It may all sound like hard work but it really isn't. Artichokes are delicious and I would hate for you to miss out on the experience!

Savoury Vegetable Couscous

SERVES 4–6

VEGAN

Vegetables

1 red capsicum (pepper), seeded and cut into small chunks
1 red onion, chopped in small pieces
1 large zucchini (courgette), cut into small chunks
4 unpeeled cloves garlic, left whole
salt
2 tablespoons extra-virgin olive oil

Couscous

230 g (8 oz) couscous
1 clove garlic, finely grated
1 teaspoon ground cumin
1 teaspoon ground turmeric
1 teaspoon ground coriander
½ teaspoon ground ginger
¼–½ teaspoon cayenne pepper
125 g (4 oz) sultanas or raisins
salt to taste
1 tablespoon extra-virgin olive oil
juice of ½ a lemon
320 ml (11 fl oz) hot water

Note: This dish is ideal as a meal on its own or as a side dish.

Garnish

400 g (14 oz) can chickpeas (garbanzos), drained
2 carrots, grated
½ cup chopped flat-leaf parsley, chopped
½ cup chopped coriander
½ cup chopped mint
salt and freshly ground black pepper
60 g (2 oz) toasted pine nuts or flaked almonds, to garnish
½ pomegranate, de-seeded, to garnish

Preheat oven to 200°C (400°F).

To prepare the vegetables, place all the ingredients in a roasting pan, toss well and roast for about 15–20 minutes until charred and tender. Vegetables should be charred but still have a bit of a bite to them.

Prepare the couscous by mixing all the ingredients together in a large bowl, cover with plastic wrap and set aside until the vegetables come out of the oven.

Gently separate and fluff the couscous with a fork, toss in the roasted vegetables then add the chickpeas, carrots, herbs, salt and pepper. Gently mix everything together, taste and adjust the seasoning, then transfer to a serving platter. Garnish with the pine nuts/almonds and pomegranate seeds.

Savoury Polenta Cake

SERVES 6

SUITABLE FOR GRAZING BOARD

150 g (5 oz) self-raising flour
½ teaspoon bicarb soda
½ teaspoon baking powder
250 g (8 oz) fine polenta
1 teaspoon dried oregano
1 teaspoon chopped rosemary
4 shallots (scallions/spring onions), finely sliced
90 g (3 oz) pitted kalamata olives
90 g (3 oz) chargrilled peppers (sliced)
60 g (2 oz) sun-dried tomatoes (sliced)
1 bunch chives, finely chopped
salt and freshly ground black pepper
350 ml (11½ fl oz) buttermilk
2 cloves garlic, finely chopped
2 extra-large eggs
60 ml (2 fl oz) extra-virgin olive oil

Balsamic vinaigrette

125 ml extra-virgin olive oil
2–3 tablespoons balsamic vinegar
salt and freshly ground black pepper
finely chopped chives

Preheat the oven to 200°C (400°F) and brush a non-stick ring cake tin liberally with extra-virgin olive oil and sprinkle all over with a little polenta.

Sift the flour, bicarb soda and baking powder into a large bowl then add the polenta, oregano, rosemary and mix well. Stir in the shallots, olives, peppers, sun-dried tomatoes and chives and season with salt and pepper.

Whisk together the buttermilk, garlic, eggs and oil, pour into the dry ingredients and mix well. Pour into the prepared cake tin and bake for 25–35 minutes until golden and a skewer comes out clean. Cool in the tin for about 10 minutes before tipping out onto a wire rack.

Meanwhile, whisk all the ingredients for the vinaigrette together.

To serve, slice the polenta cake and serve warm with a drizzle of the vinaigrette.

Note: You can make this recipe into muffins to serve individually. Great on a grazing board.

Eggplant with Chickpeas

SERVES 4

VEGAN

4 tablespoons olive oil
1 eggplant (aubergine), approx. 500 g (18 oz), cubed
1 large onion, finely chopped
3 cloves garlic, finely chopped
1½ teaspoons ground cumin
1 teaspoon ground turmeric
1 teaspoon chilli flakes
2 ripe tomatoes, skinned and chopped
2 x 400 g (14 oz) cans chickpeas (garbanzos), drained and rinsed
zest of 1 lime or lemon
250 ml (8 fl oz) hot water
salt
handful of chopped fresh coriander (cilantro) including stalks
Greek yoghurt (optional)
lemon/lime juice

Heat the oil in a large frying pan and cook the eggplant until golden. Add the onion and continue cooking until soft. You may need to add a little more oil as the eggplant tends to absorb oil quickly.

Stir in the garlic, cumin, turmeric and chilli and cook for about 30 seconds. Add the tomatoes, chickpeas, zest and water, season with salt, cover and simmer on low heat for 10 minutes. Add more water to the pan if it starts to dry out too much. Stir in the coriander and cook for another 2–3 minutes before serving with some Greek yoghurt and a squeeze of lime or lemon juice.

Moroccan Chickpea and Vegetable Tagine

SERVES 4–6

VEGAN

3 tablespoons extra-virgin olive oil
1 large onion, chopped
4 cloves garlic, chopped
2 medium carrots, sliced
400 g (14 oz) can diced tomatoes
2 x 400 g (14 oz) cans chickpeas (garbanzos), drained
320 ml (11 fl oz) water
2 zucchini (courgettes), diced
250 g (8 oz) cauliflower florets
250 g (8 oz) frozen whole baby beans
125 g (4 oz) baby spinach leaves
Greek yoghurt, lime juice and chopped fresh coriander (optional), to serve

Moroccan spice mix

1 tablespoons ground cumin
2 teaspoons paprika
1 x 2.5 cm (1 in) piece fresh turmeric, grated
1 teaspoon ground ginger
1 teaspoon allspice
¼ teaspoon cinnamon
½–1 teaspoon dried chilli flakes
2 teaspoons salt

Mix all the spice ingredients together and set aside.

Heat the oil in a large saucepan over medium heat and cook the onion until soft and golden. Add the garlic and cook until fragrant. Stir in the spice mix and cook for about a minute to release the fragrant oils but be careful not to burn. Add a little more oil if the pan is too dry. Add the carrots, tomatoes, chickpeas and water, bring to the boil, reduce the heat, cover and simmer for 20 minutes. Stir in the zucchini, cauliflower, frozen beans and cook for a further 10–12 minutes. Stir in the spinach leaves, take off the heat and leave covered for 10 minutes until the spinach has wilted.

Serve over couscous with a dollop of yoghurt, lime juice and fresh coriander.

Vegetable Caponata

SERVES 4

VEGAN

4 tablespoons extra-virgin olive oil
1 large eggplant (aubergine), about 600 g (21 oz), cut into cubes
1 red onion, chopped
3 cloves garlic, finely chopped
400 g (14 oz) can diced tomatoes
½ teaspoon sugar
90 g (3 oz) stuffed green olives
2 tablespoons capers
2 teaspoons dried oregano
salt and freshly ground black pepper
2 tablespoons red wine vinegar
large handful finely chopped flat-leaf parsley

Heat the oil in a large frying pan until hot, add the eggplant and cook on high heat until browned. You may need to add a little more oil as the eggplant tends to absorb oil very quickly. Add the onion and cook until soft. Stir in all the remaining ingredients except the parsley. Reduce the heat and simmer for about 15 minutes.

Stir in the parsley, cook for another 1–2 minutes and adjust the seasoning if necessary.

Note: This is a lovely vegetable dish that can be eaten warm or cold. It is delicious served with rice and as an accompaniment with meat, chicken or fish.

Mum's Spinach Pie with Rice

SERVES 6

VEGAN

650 g (23 oz) store-bought frozen puff pastry,
or 4 sheets ready rolled
150 g (5 oz) medium grain rice
1 large bunch silverbeet spinach
1 teaspoon salt
1 medium onion, grated
6 shallots (scallions/spring onions), finely sliced
125 ml (4 fl oz) extra-virgin olive oil
freshly ground black pepper
sesame seeds

Note: This is my mother's famous spinach pie, a favourite with my family. She used to make it often for my children as she knew how much they loved it. It's still a huge favourite to this day except I now make it for my children and their children.

Thaw the pastry to room temperature.

Soak the rice in boiling water for 15 minutes then drain well.

Discard the big, tough lower stalks from the spinach and chop the leaves into smallish pieces, including the smaller tender parts of the stalks. Wash the spinach really well and put it in a colander with the salt. Using your hands gently rub and squeeze the salt into the spinach to allow it to penetrate the leaves. Leave to stand in the colander for 5–10 minutes then squeeze to remove any excess moisture. The spinach will have collapsed in volume.

Preheat the oven to 200°C (400°F) and lightly grease a 30 x 24 cm (12 x 9½ in) baking dish with olive oil.

Place the spinach in a bowl with the rice, onion, shallots, oil and pepper and mix well.

Roll out two sheets of pastry to fit the prepared dish or, if using ready rolled pastry, arrange two sheets of ready rolled pastry on the bottom and up the sides of the baking dish (they will overlap in the centre). Spread the spinach mixture on top, cover with the remaining pastry sheets, cut off any excess pastry and crimp the edges together. Prick the top of the pastry all over with a fork to create air vents, brush with olive oil and scatter sesame seeds on top. Bake for 50–60 minutes until golden.

Chickpeas with Spinach and Mushrooms

SERVES 4

VEGAN

2 tablespoons olive oil
1 cinnamon stick
1 tablespoon cumin seeds
1 red onion, finely chopped
2 cloves garlic, finely chopped
1 red chilli, chopped, or dried chilli flakes to taste
2 teaspoons ground turmeric or 1 tablespoon grated fresh turmeric
1 teaspoon ground coriander
2 teaspoons ground cumin
350 g (12 oz) mushrooms, sliced
400 g (14 oz) can diced tomatoes
2 x 400 g (14 oz) cans chickpeas (garbanzos), undrained
200 g (7 oz) baby spinach leaves
salt to taste
2 tablespoons chopped coriander
lime juice
Greek yoghurt, or vegan substitute (optional)

Heat the oil in a large saucepan over medium heat, stir in the cinnamon stick and cumin seeds and cook until fragrant. Add the onion and cook until soft. Stir in the garlic, chilli, turmeric, coriander and cumin and cook for a minute. Add the mushrooms and cook 2–5 minutes until the mushrooms soften. Stir in the tomatoes and chickpeas and simmer, covered, for 10–15 minutes, stirring occasionally. Add the spinach, season with salt and simmer for a further 2–3 minutes until the spinach has wilted, then stir in the coriander.

Serve with rice, a sprinkle of lime juice and yoghurt.

Baked Roasted Capsicum, Spinach, Olive and Cheese Frittata

SERVES 4–6

SUITABLE FOR GRAZING BOARD

150 g (5 oz) baby spinach leaves
150 g (5 oz) roasted capsicum (pepper), chopped
15 pitted kalamata olives, halved
4 shallots (scallions/spring onions), sliced
1 clove garlic, grated
125 g (4 oz) feta or goats cheese, crumbled
150 g (5 oz) ricotta cheese
3 tablespoons grated parmesan cheese
10 extra-large eggs, beaten
freshly ground pepper
salt

Preheat the oven to 200°C (400°F) and lightly grease a 23 x 6 cm (9 x 3 in) square baking dish. Line the dish with a sheet of non-stick baking paper, making sure the sides overhang to make it easier to lift out the frittata.

Place the spinach in a bowl with the roasted capsicum, olives, shallots, garlic, feta, ricotta and parmesan cheese. Pour in the beaten eggs, season with pepper and a little salt and mix well. You may not need to add salt as the olives and cheese can be salty.

Pour the mixture into the prepared dish and bake for about 30–40 minutes or until the frittata is set and a skewer comes out clean when tested. Leave to cool slightly for about 5 minutes before serving.

Note: This frittata is also lovely eaten cold and suitable for picnics. It can also be prepared as individual muffins, which will take 20–25 minutes to cook.

Yellow Split Pea Puree

SERVES 4

VEGAN

500 g (18 oz) yellow split peas
1 litre (32 fl oz) water
1 medium brown onion, finely chopped
3–4 cloves garlic, finely chopped
3 tablespoons extra-virgin olive oil
salt and freshly ground black pepper
lemon juice, to serve
chopped onion, to serve

Place split peas in a sieve and rinse under cold running water until the water runs clear. Drain well and place in a large saucepan with the water, onion, garlic and a tablespoon of olive oil. Bring to the boil, reduce the heat and simmer for 40–45 minutes until almost all of the water is absorbed. Skim off any froth that comes to the surface during cooking.

Remove from the heat, pour in the remaining oil, season with salt and pepper and, using a wooden spoon, stir vigorously until you have a thick puree with texture. Taste and adjust the seasoning and serve with a drizzle of extra-virgin olive oil, lemon juice, chopped onion and lots of fresh crusty bread.

Note: This is a dish enjoyed in Greece called 'Fava'. It is very easy and quick to make, thick and perfect comfort food. Any leftovers set very firm in the fridge but heat through beautifully. If you find it too thick add a little water.

Acknowledgements

I cannot put into words how grateful I am for the love and support that has been shown to me over the last few years from my New Holland family, wonderful friends and my own very precious family.

To Fiona Schultz and all the staff at New Holland, a very special thank you for your constant support, understanding, patience and for allowing me to continue being part of your family.

A special thank you to my wonderful publishing and production manager Arlene Gippert, for all your help and guidance in putting this book together. It has been a real joy to work with you; you have made it very easy for me.

Thank you also to my editor Liz Hardy for all your hard work and to Andrew Davies for designing and creating such a beautiful book, it is much appreciated.

I would also like to thank my dear friends Linda Williams and Victor Yoog, formerly at New Holland for the many years of unswaying support and friendship.

To two very important and talented people, my wonderful stylist Georgie Dolling and photographer Joe Filshie (our second book together Joe), thank you both so much for making the photo shoot such a breeze and for bringing my home cooking to life. Without the gorgeous photos and beautiful styling this book would not be what it is.

To my beautiful and loving family: my children Alex, Nikki and Christopher, their other halves Lachlan, Marcus and Carolyn and to my very precious grandchildren, Madison, Kobe, Isaac, Hudson, Cooper, Brooklyn, Bailey, Chloe and Keira, all I can say is thank you and I love you.

Lastly to all my wonderful and caring friends who have never left my side,
Thank you ***x***.

Index

Artichoke Hearts with Broad Beans and Lemon 194
Artichoke, Olive and Broccoli Pasta Salad 73
Asparagus with Prosciutto, Dijon Mustard and Parmesan 54
Baba Ganoush (Eggplant/Aubergine Dip) 33
Baked Cabbage Rolls 125
Baked Chicken with Oregano and Garlic 179
Baked Kibbeh 121
Baked Meatballs 124
Baked Roasted Capsicum, Spinach, Olive and Cheese Frittata 220
Baked Shoulder of Lamb with Risoni 100
Bean Patties with Yoghurt and Mint Sauce 202
Beef Pot Roast in Red Wine 102
Black-Eyed Bean Soup 23
Black-Eyed Beans with Cumin and Potatoes 207
Borlotti Bean and Vegetable Soup 27
Borlotti Bean, Rocket and Tomato Salad 74
Brown Lentil and Spinach Soup 21
Cauliflower Patties 201
Cauliflower Soup 24
Chicken Cacciatore 167
Chicken Kebabs with Garlic, Coriander and Lime 175
Chicken Livers and Pancetta in Marsala Wine 184
Chicken Tagine with Olives and Preserved Lemon 178
Chicken with Leeks and Mustard Sauce 183
Chicken in Wine and Chestnuts 170
Chickpea (Garbanzo), Olive and Feta Salad 57
Chickpeas (Garbanzos) with Spinach and Mushrooms 219
Chorizo Sausage Antipasto 104
Chorizo Sausage, Pepper and Olive Frittata 122
Creamy Polenta 78
Crispy Pita Triangles 49
Crumbed Fresh Sardines 145
Eggplant (Aubergine) Moussaka 114
Eggplant Parmigiana 195
Eggplant with Chickpeas (Garbanzos) 214
Egyptian Molokhia Soup 19
Fattoush Salad 68
Felafel 204
Fennel Baked Potatoes 198
Foccacia Bread 50
Fried Calamari 146
Garlic and Chilli Prawn Linguine 88
Garlic Prawns 137
Greek Baked Potatoes 199
Greek Lamb Cutlets 99
Grilled Baby Octopus 149
Grilled Broccoli and Fennel Salad 63
Herbed Roast Chicken with 40 Cloves of Garlic 182
Hummus 30
Italian Chicken Parcels 171
Italian Pizza Loaf 38
Kale, Bean, Sun-dried Tomato and Artichoke Salad 56
Kofta Kebabs 110
Lamb Souvlakia 109
Legumes and Chilli Salad with Lime and Fresh Coriander 62
Lentil Pilaf 79
Liver with Rosemary 107
Meat Loaf 106
Mediterranean Salami and Bocconcini Pide Bread Fingers 46
Middle Eastern Spiced Lentils with Spinach 203
Moroccan Baked Fish with Preserved Lemons 150
Moroccan Chickpea and Vegetable Tagine 215
Moroccan Roast Chicken 176
Mum's Spinach Pie with Rice 218
Mushroom and Prosciutto Risotto 94
Mussels in White Wine and Herbs 153
Mustard and Dill Crusted Salmon 157
Octopus in Red Wine 133
Olive Bread 45
Olive, Spinach and Feta Twist 37
Osso Bucco 113
Oysters with Chilli, Garlic Herb Butter and Parmesan Cheese 158
Pancetta and Bocconcini Pasta Bake 81
Pan-Grilled Calamari 161
Pasta and Kale Salad 75
Pasta with Chorizo Sausage, Olives and Sun-Dried Tomatoes 85
Penne with Yoghurt and Caramelised Onions 83
Persian Eggs with Lentils and Spinach 206
Pickled Octopus 142
Pizza Wheels 42
Porcini Mushroom Risotto 87
Potato and Tomato Salad 67
Prawns with Charmoula 134
Prawns with Feta 130
Prosciutto, Buffalo Mozzarella and Fig Salad 61
Pumpkin, Lentil and Spinach Soup 20
Quick Cheese Pie 189
Quick Tomato, Herb and Chilli Pasta Sauce 82
Quinoa Tabouleh 69
Rice with Turmeric, Leek and Lentils 95
Ricotta, Olive and Basil Tart with Tomatoes 35
Roast Pumpkin, Spinach and Lentil Salad 58
Rustic Beef, Vegetable and Cracked Wheat Soup 17
Salade Niçoise 72
Salt Cod Fritters 129
Savoury Polenta Cake 213
Savoury Vegetable Couscous 211
Seafood Marinara Sauce 154
Seafood Skewers 162
Shakshuka 190
Slow Cooked Lamb 117
Spaghettini alle Vongole 91
Spaghetti with Lemon 92
Spaghetti with Mushrooms and Garlic 86
Spanish Chicken with Rice and Chorizo 180
Spanish Prawns 140
Spiced Red Lentil Soup 26
Spicy Chicken Wings 172
Spicy Moroccan Lamb 118
Spinach and Rice in Red Sauce 193
Steak and Lentil Salad 71
Stuffed Artichokes 210
Stuffed Chicken Breasts in a Red Wine Mushroom Sauce 168
Stuffed Tomatoes with Mince and Rice 103
Summer Pasta Salad 64
Sun-Dried Tomato, Herb and Garlic Cheese Ball 41
Tomato and Basil Soup 18
Tzatziki (Cucumber Dip) 34
Vegetable Caponata 216
Whitebait 138
Whole Calamari with Savoury Rice 141
Whole Snapper with Herbed Rice and Mushrooms 132
Yellow Split Pea Puree 221
Zucchini (Courgette) and Haloumi Fritters 209
Zucchini (Courgette) Potato and Herb Tortilla 197

First published in 2024 by New Holland Publishers
Sydney

Level 1, 178 Fox Valley Road, Wahroonga, NSW 2076, Australia

newhollandpublishers.com

A record of this book is held at the National Library of Australia.

ISBN 9781760794095

Managing Director: Fiona Schultz
Project Editor: Liz Hardy
Designer: Andrew Davies
Photographer: Joe Filshie
Stylist: Georgie Dolling
Production Director: Arlene Gippert
Printed in China

Keep up with New Holland Publishers:
NewHollandPublishers
@newhollandpublishers

Photography credits:

All photos by Joe Filshie
except pages 31, 32, 43, 48, 51, 55, 120, 123, 128, 135, 147, 159, 160, 163, 185, 196, 200, 205, 208, 217 by Graeme Gillies
and page 12 from Shutterstock